Langston Hughes

Mitchell Lane
PUBLISHERS

P.O. Box 196
Hockessin, Delaware 19707

Poets and Playwrights

Carl Sandburg

Emily Dickinson

Langston Hughes

Tennessee Williams

William Shakespeare

Langston Hughes

Karen Gibson

Printing   1   2   3   4   5   6   7   8   9

Library of Congress Cataloging-in-Publication Data
   Gibson, Karen Bush.
      Langston Hughes / by Karen Bush Gibson.
         p. cm. — (Poets and playwrights)
      Includes bibliographical references and index.
      ISBN 1-58415-431-4 (library bound : alk. paper)
    1. Hughes, Langston, 1902–1967—Juvenile literature. 2. African-American poets—Biography—Juvenile literature. 3. Poets, American—20th century—Biography—Juvenile literature. I. Title. II. Series.
      PS3515.U274Z643 2006
      818'.5209—dc22
                             2005036700

ISBN-13: 9781584154310

ABOUT THE AUTHOR: Karen Bush Gibson has written extensively for the juvenile educational market. Her work has included biographies, current events, and cultural histories, such as *The Life and Times of Catherine the Great, The Fury of Hurricane Andrew,* and *The Life and Times of John Peter Zenger* for Mitchell Lane Publishers.

PHOTO CREDITS: Cover, pp. 1, 3—Library of Congress; pp. 6, 12, 22—Yale Collection of American Literature, Beinecke Rare Book and Manuscript Library; pp. 34— Library of Congress; p. 44—Superstock; p. 55—Yale Collection of American Literature, Beinecke Rare Book and Manuscript Library; p. 64—Getty Images; pp. 72, 75, 82, 90— Yale Collection of American Literature, Beinecke Rare Book and Manuscript Library.

PUBLISHER'S NOTE: This story is based on the author's extensive research, which she believes to be accurate. Documentation of such research is contained on page 107.

    The internet sites referenced herein were active as of the publication date. Due to the fleeting nature of some web sites, we cannot guarantee they will all be active when you are reading this book.

PLB

Contents

*For Your Information

The *Weary Blues* was Langston Hughes's first published book. The title of this poetry collection was taken from a prizewinning poem of the same name.

Chapter

1

"The Weary Blues"

Langston Hughes sat the banquet table, wishing he had stayed home in Washington, D.C. He was still recovering from a bout of malaria probably caught from his trip to Africa. The twenty-four-year-old was tired and broke, but Jessie Fauset, sitting next to him, had insisted he come. She had even loaned him the train fare to get to New York City. She was the first person to publish his work, and Hughes felt much gratitude to the literary editor of *The Crisis,* a magazine published by the National Association for the Advancement of Colored People (NAACP).

They sat at a fancy Fifth Avenue restaurant in downtown Manhattan, a place unlike anything Hughes had seen before. The banquet was for a literary contest hosted by the magazine *Opportunity: A Journal of Negro Life.* The National Urban League's monthly magazine had gained a lot of notice in the two years it had been published. Soon, the results of the first *Opportunity* literary contest would be revealed, with $500 in prizes being awarded for poetry, short stories, plays, and essays. As they waited, Fauset pointed out people from major publishing houses like Alfred A. Knopf and Harper and Brothers.

Hughes had entered several of his poems in the contest. At the last minute, he decided to include "The Weary Blues," a poem he had written three years before while working on a ship on the Hudson River. The poem was about a man in Harlem who sang the blues all night. Included was the first blues verse Hughes had ever heard while growing up in Lawrence, Kansas. The poem captured the rhythm of the music Hughes enjoyed so much. He had revised "The Weary Blues" since then, particularly the ending. Finally, deciding that there was nothing more he could do with it, he entered it in the contest. It was one of 730 entries being read by judges that included playwright Eugene O'Neill and other literary giants.

Excitement was building in the upscale restaurant. The *Opportunity* awards were the first occasion to bring talented African American writers together with influential white publishers and editors. According to noted Hughes biographer Arnold Rampersad, "Virtually all the younger black writers, shiny-faced with anticipation, were present, including Hughes's former friend and his main poetical arch-rival Countee Cullen, who had been publishing with such dazzling authority that in the previous November alone he had placed poems in four different white journals."[1]

Hughes sat up straighter and smiled when he and Countee Cullen were announced as tied for third place in the poetry competition. Hughes had won for "America" and also received honorable mentions for two other poems. He congratulated Cullen, who also won the second-place prize for a poem titled "To One Who Said Me Nay."

"And the winner of the first prize for poetry in the *Opportunity* Magazine Literary contest is . . . Langston Hughes for his poem, 'The Weary Blues.'" Hughes was shocked as people patted him on the back and shook his hand. Did he think of his parents at all in those moments after hearing his name announced? The only thing James Hughes and Carrie Langston Hughes had ever agreed on besides getting a divorce was that their only child was wasting his time with this writing business. Perhaps the woman who had raised him for most of his first twelve years would have understood. His grandmother, Mary Langston, had told him that it was his responsibility to achieve important things someday, just as his ancestors had.

After the announcement of the awards, the crowd mingled. Drinks in hand, they greeted old friends and made new acquaintances. Fauset introduced Hughes around the room. He met *Opportunity* editor Charles S. Johnson. Johnson had put the *Opportunity* contest and banquet together to publicize promising African American writers. Hughes met others, including a young unknown writer, Zora Neale Hurston, who had won the short story prize. A man named Carl Van Vechten, whom Hughes had met six months earlier at an NAACP benefit, walked up and congratulated him. Van Vechten, a supporter of the arts, asked Hughes if he had enough poems for a book. He said he had and agreed to send them to Van Vechten when he returned home to Washington, D.C.

The forty-dollar prize was much needed, but just as satisfying was hearing author and editor James Weldon Johnson read the prizewinning poem that would become the title of the first of seventeen volumes of poetry by Hughes. Johnson's voice rang out over the room as he captured the rhythm that began "The Weary Blues."

> *Droning a drowsy syncopated tune,*
> *Rocking back and forth to a mellow croon,*
> *I heard a Negro play.*
> *Down on Lenox Avenue the other night*
> *By the pale dull pallor of an old gas light*
> *He did a lazy sway . . .*
> *He did a lazy sway . . .*
> *To the tune o' those Weary Blues.*[2]

Some considered the night Hughes won the National Urban League's *Opportunity* Magazine Poetry Prize—May 1, 1925—as the birth of the Harlem Renaissance. Langston Hughes, at the age of twenty-four, was a leader of this African American cultural movement. In 1980, African American literature expert Charles H. Nichols wrote: "Langston Hughes is without rival as the most prolific and influential Afro-American writer in our history."[3]

Langston Hughes was a poet, novelist, short story writer, nonfiction writer, playwright, and lyricist. In his first autobiography, *The Big Sea,* he said that for him, "words turned into songs, plays, scenarios, articles, and stories."[4] He opened doors for himself and for other writers by showing people that it was possible for an African American to be a successful writer without compromising his principles. His writing addressed the concerns and culture of his race with dignity. Among his innovative verse were lines of poetry that sounded like blues or jazz rhythms. He was a respected writer and one of the greatest poets of the twentieth century.

The Harlem Renaissance

The Harlem Renaissance began in the 1920s as a period of intense cultural activity by African American people. Essayist and educator Alain Locke first drew attention to this movement when he published an anthology of works by African American writers titled *The New Negro*. People began calling this cultural phenomenon the New Negro Movement. *The New York Herald Tribune* may have been the first to use the term *Negro Renaissance* when it compared the *Opportunity* literary contest, in which Hughes won the first place poetry prize, to the European Renaissance of the fifteenth and sixteenth centuries that resulted in an explosion of creative activity. *Harlem Renaissance* was later adopted because of the largely African American community of Harlem in upper Manhattan of New York City, where many writers, musicians, and artists lived.

One of the factors that contributed to the Harlem Renaissance was the migration of African Americans to northern cities like New York, Chicago, and Washington, D.C. Away from the more segregated society of the South, intellectual development soared. The previous generation had been the first to be born free of slavery. Additionally, this generation—the parents of many of Hughes's generation—was the first to be granted the right to vote when the Fifteenth Amendment was ratified by Congress in 1870. It was a time of great social change. Locke described the movement as a "spiritual emancipation." In 1925, he and James Weldon Johnson wrote "Harlem: Mecca of the New Negro" about the talent of the African American community for a special issue of a monthly magazine for professionals called *Survey Graphic*.

Like Hughes, many writers of the Harlem Renaissance wrote poetry, but there was also a great deal of short stories, plays, novels, and nonfiction. Jessie Fauset was a poet, short story writer, and novelist. One of her best known works was *The Chinaberry Tree; A Novel of American Life*. Even more important was her work as a literary editor who encouraged writers like Hughes. Hughes believed that Fauset, Locke, and Charles S. Johnson were the three people who aided the Harlem Renaissance in giving birth to such talented writers as Zora Neale Hurston, Claude McKay, Countee Cullen, and Jean Toomer. Hurston was an authority on African American culture and author of the novel *Their Eyes Were Watching God*. The Jamaican poet Claude McKay published *Harlem Shadows*, one of the earlier books of poetry during this period. Poet Countee Cullen probably won more awards for his poetry than any other poet in the 1920s. Jean Toomer was a noted nonfiction writer who released a collection of short stories, sketches, poetry, and a play, *Cane* (1923), which was described by critics as one of the best examples of Harlem Renaissance literature. Many literary critics place Langston Hughes at the forefront of the Harlem Renaissance. Poet, prose writer, novelist, short story writer, lyricist—there seemed to be no literary style he couldn't master as he paved the way for other African American writers.

African American creativity flourished in other areas as well. Music, particularly the blues and jazz, reached new heights in popularity, with bandleader W.C. Handy and singer Bessie Smith playing to audiences of all races. Opera singer Marion Anderson, actor/singer Paul Robeson, and dancer Bill Robinson were popular African American entertainers. *Shuffle Along* became the first musical revue written and performed by African Americans, opening on Broadway in 1921. It would take fourteen more years before *Porgy and Bess,* with its all–African American cast, opened on Broadway. New York would also launch the innovative talents of musicians like Louis Armstrong and Duke Ellington. By 1934, Harlem's Apollo Theater would feature professional and amateur African American musicians. Meanwhile the world of sports introduced boxer Joe Louis and runner Jesse Owens. In a time when African Americans were rarely allowed to play basketball, the Harlem Globetrotters team was established in 1927.

W.C. Handy

The Harlem Renaissance became more than a literary movement by helping to break down walls of racism through the achievements of African Americans. Joel E. Spingarn of the NAACP began awarding a medal each year, beginning in 1914, to the African American person who achieved the most. This included not only people in literature, but in politics, science, and sports. The award continues to be awarded by the board of directors of the NAACP.

When the stock market crashed in 1929, bringing the Great Depression to America, interest in the Harlem Renaissance faded. Yet the major contributions to American literature and music from the Harlem Renaissance are still felt in the twenty-first century.

11

Langston Hughes with his mother during happier times in 1916. Carrie Hughes Clark moved frequently during Langston's childhood, often leaving him with his grandmother.

Chapter 2

Growing Up in Kansas

Early in the twentieth century, Joplin, Missouri, was a booming town where men came to work in the lead mines. It was in Joplin that James Langston Hughes was born February 1, 1902, to James and Carrie Hughes. James had been working as a bookkeeper for a mining company. The name the child would be known as for the rest of his life was his middle name (after his mother's maiden name): Langston. Although less than three years old by the time of Langston's birth, the Hughes marriage was already in trouble. James and Carrie could not have been any more different.

Carolyn Mercer Langston, known as Carrie, grew up as the only daughter of Charles and Mary Langston in the progressive town of Lawrence in the new Kansas Territory. When Kansas Territory opened for settlement in 1854, the laws of the time dictated that settlers could decide whether to admit their territory as a slave state or a free state. Abolitionists rushed in and started the town of Lawrence in an effort to make Kansas into a free state. Lawrence became an important stop on the Underground Railroad, helping slaves reach freedom.

Carrie, who was popular in school, enjoyed performing in front of others. Encouraged by her father, she read her own poems for the Kansas Inter-State Literary Society while she was a high school student. Before she graduated from high school, her father died. Money had never meant much to the politically active Charles Langston, an important civic leader in Lawrence, but after he died, money became tight. Charles left a heavily mortgaged home to his wife and daughter. Carrie worked as a clerk in the district court to help support herself and her mother. The strain became worse as she and her mother began fighting. Carrie enjoyed going out and having fun. She especially loved musical theater and hoped to be an actress one day. Mary Langston believed that music other than hymns was shameful. She said the same about theater and novels. Carrie wanted to leave her mother's home.

After taking a teaching course at Kansas State Normal School in Emporia, Carrie traveled south to Oklahoma Territory in 1898. She was to teach at a school in the territorial capital of Guthrie. With the recent land run in Oklahoma Territory, many towns, including Guthrie, had been settled in a single day. Carrie was excited to be living only twelve miles away from what the *New York Times* called a "black mecca." Founded in 1890, the town of Langston, named after Carrie's uncle John, was planned as an all–African American town. It was the center of African American culture for the area. After settlers bought land for a school, the Presbyterian Church opened the Colored Agricultural and Normal University in 1898. It would be renamed Langston University, and today it is a leader in agricultural research.

It was in Langston that Carrie met an ambitious storekeeper named James Nathaniel Hughes. James's father had fought in the Civil War and was a successful farmer in Charlestown, Indiana, until his death when James was sixteen. His two brothers had been respected Buffalo Soldiers with the all–African American regiments that safeguarded the frontier. Both of James's grandfathers were white men from Kentucky. Interracial relationships were common in the late nineteenth century. Biracial children from these unions had the same limited rights that other African Americans did at the time. Most likely this treatment contributed to James's bitter and unhappy outlook on life.

Only two years older than Carrie, James had already worked as a teacher, law clerk, farmer, and homesteader. What he really wanted to be was a lawyer. He had studied the law, but as an African American, he was prohibited from taking the bar exam in most places, including Oklahoma Territory. Angry at the unfair system, James spoke against poor minorities, particularly African Americans. He seemed to believe that poor people brought on their unfortunate circumstances. In *Langston Hughes, Before and Beyond Harlem,* author Faith Berry writes of Langston's father: "In his father's oft-spoken opinion, blacks had only themselves to blame for their dismal poverty and powerlessness."[1]

James and Carrie married in Guthrie on April 30, 1899, with no family present. A few months later, a pregnant Carrie and her husband moved to

Joplin to find a job James could be happy with. The infant died soon after birth. Husband and wife moved to Buffalo, New York, for a while, but returned to Joplin while Carrie was pregnant with Langston. James Hughes's frustration mounted as he decided he would never get the opportunities he deserved in the United States. He talked about moving to Cuba, where he had heard that African Americans were treated fairly. He may have gone there for a short time, but soon after Langston's birth, he moved to Mexico City, where he worked as a confidential secretary to the general manager of the Pullman Train Company.

For the first years of his life, Langston moved from place to place with his mother. They lived with Mary Langston in Lawrence, then with his aunt Sarita in Indianapolis for a while. They lived in New York and Colorado. When necessary, Langston lived with his grandmother in Lawrence. Soon after turning five or six, he lived in Mexico City as his parents tried to reconcile. A major earthquake hit the city. For Carrie, this was the last straw, and she immediately left for the United States with Langston. James remained in Mexico. The marriage was over, and Langston wouldn't see his father again for eleven years.

Langston remembered living in Topeka, Kansas, when he was six years old. He and his mother rented a room over a plumbing shop in the white business district. Money was scarce, and Langston remembered his mother being angry at his father for leaving her with a child to raise alone. Langston contributed by searching the alleys and streets for wooden boxes to take home. Carrie would break up the boxes to burn in the stove they used for heating and cooking.

It wasn't all hardships, though. Langston later recalled being introduced to two things in Topeka that changed his life forever: music and the public library. "In Topeka, as a small child, my mother took me with her to the little vine-covered library on the rounds of the Capitol. There I first fell in love with librarians, and I have been in love with them ever since—those very nice women who help you find wonderful books!"[2]

Langston was excited when it finally came time to enter first grade. Although the closest school to their home was Harrison Street School, it welcomed only white students. Carrie was told to go across town and enroll her son in Washington School. She argued that the school for African Americans was too far away for a six-year-old to walk to while she was at work. She appealed to the school board and won. Langston was allowed to enroll in the Harrison Street School. Interestingly, one of the most important battles for school integration would be fought fifty years later with the Topeka School Board.

As the only African American student at the school, Langston occasionally endured cruel comments from students, and even from a teacher. Langston said in his first autobiography, *The Big Sea*, that "all the teachers were nice to me, except one who sometimes used to make remarks about my being colored. And after such remarks, occasionally the kids would grab stones and tin cans out of the alley and chase me home."[3]

Langston was a bright child and a model student. When April rolled around, Carrie pulled him from Harrison Street School and moved him to Lawrence, Kansas, to live with his grandmother. "And my mother, who worked, always traveled about a great deal, looking for a better job,"[4] he wrote. Although he would live with his mother briefly in Colorado and Kansas City, the remainder of his early childhood was spent in Lawrence with Mary Sampson Patterson Leary Langston.

The only thing stable in young Langston's life was his grandmother. Almost seventy when her grandson was born, Mary Langston took after her Native American ancestors with her copper skin and long black hair. Born as a free woman in North Carolina, her heritage included African American, French, and Cherokee. She met her first husband, Lewis Sheridan Leary, at Oberlin College. Together, they helped people escape to the North through the Underground Railroad. Operated by abolitionists and free African Americans, the Underground Railroad was a way of helping slaves escape to the North. It wasn't really a railroad. People used railroad terms as code words. For example, people like Mary and her husband were called conductors. The Underground Railroad may have helped up to 100,000 people escape slavery. It also inspired the revolutionary book *Uncle Tom's Cabin*. Written by American abolitionist Harriet Beecher Stowe in 1852, *Uncle Tom's Cabin* was a best-selling novel about slavery that influenced other abolitionists. The character of Uncle Tom was that of an obedient African American slave. The popularity of *Uncle Tom's Cabin* continued on stage. Langston called it the "most cussed and discussed book of its time."[5]

Without telling Mary, Leary joined abolitionist John Brown in an attack on the federal armory at Harpers Ferry in Virginia (now part of West Virginia). He was shot dead. Langston later wrote about the stories his grandmother told about her first husband. "My grandmother said Sheridan Leary always did believe people should be free."[6] Mary kept the shawl in which Leary died close to her for the rest of her life. Sometimes she used the shawl—with its bullet holes—to cover young Langston. When Langston was eight years old, his grandmother took him to Osawatomie, Kansas, on the last day of August for the dedication of the John Brown Memorial Battlefield. Former President Theodore Roosevelt honored her as the last surviving widow from the Harpers Ferry incident.

In 1869, after ten years as a widow, Mary married Charles Langston, son of a prosperous white plantation owner and a former slave who worked recruiting African Americans for the 54th and 55th Massachusetts regiments in the Civil War. Although it was illegal for them to do so, Charles's parents lived as husband and wife, and they had three sons: Gideon, Charles, and John Mercer. In the same year that Sheridan Leary participated in John Brown's raid at Harpers Ferry, Charles, who was also an abolitionist, was arrested for helping a runaway slave escape to Canada. At his trial, Charles spoke against the Fugitive Slave Law, which made it illegal to help people escape from slavery. "Let me stand in that Hall, and tell a United States Marshal that my father was a Revolutionary soldier; that he served under Lafayette, and fought through the whole war; and that he always told me that he fought for *my* freedom as much as for his own; and he would sneer at me, and clutch me with his bloody fingers, and say he had a *right* to make me a slave! And when I appeal to Congress, they say he has a right to make me a slave; when I appeal to the people, they say he has a right to make me a slave, and when I appeal to your Honor, *your Honor* says he has a right to make me a slave, and if any man, white or black, seeks an investigation of that claim, they make themselves amenable to the pains and penalties of the Fugitive Slave Act, for BLACK MEN HAVE NO RIGHTS WHICH WHITE MEN ARE BOUND TO RESPECT."[7]

The judge found Charles's speech so moving that he reduced his sentence from six months in jail with a $1,000 fine to twenty days in jail and a $100 fine.

John Mercer Langston also worked against slavery. According to Hughes biographer Arnold Rampersad, "Adding to Charles Langston's prestige was the fame of his youngest brother; John Mercer Langston was one of the three [with Frederick Douglass and Booker T. Washington] best known black Americans."[8] With three college degrees, John Mercer Langston was a lawyer who prided himself on breaking down the walls of discrimination. He was appointed to many offices, including serving as a law professor and president of Howard University in Washington, D.C. In 1890, John was elected to Congress from Virginia. He became the first African American elected to Congress from Virginia and served from 1890 to 1891.

Langston came from a family that prized education. Both his maternal grandparents studied at Oberlin College. Mary Langston was one of the first

African American women to attend the Ohio college. She read to her grandson from the Bible and from *Grimm's Fairy Tales*. But most of her stories were about courageous people working for freedom for enslaved African Americans through the Underground Railroad and at Harpers Ferry. Langston's grandmother made certain he knew that he came from great people and that great things were expected from him also. What he learned was that nobody cried in his grandmother's stories. According to Rampersad, Langston learned at an early age that there was no point to crying.

Hughes remembered his grandmother taking him as a young child to Topeka, Kansas, to hear "the greatest colored man in the world,"[9] educator Booker T. Washington, speak before a packed auditorium. Washington, a former slave, had established the Tuskegee Institute in 1881. He was perhaps the best-known African American man in the country at the time.

Langston's childhood among dominant women affected his life and his writing. In his first novel, *Not Without Laughter,* his main character, Sandy, was also raised by his grandmother in a small Kansas town.

Mary Langston had lived in the same house since 1888, but after twenty years, the racial makeup began to change in Lawrence. Segregation became a way of life in the once progressive Kansas town. The church she had attended for years began admitting only white people. Instead of fighting the decision or finding another church, she stayed at home and read her Bible. Soon her home was one of only a few African American homes in her neighborhood, located near the University of Kansas. She made Langston come straight home from school, rarely allowing him playtime in their white neighborhood.

Mary Langston didn't have much money. She refused to work as a servant for white people, one of the few jobs available to elderly African American women. Sometimes she made money by renting out her home and living with friends. The salt pork and dandelion greens that made up many of their meals wasn't very filling for a growing boy.

His grandmother was a proud and dignified woman, but she didn't seem to be very affectionate with her grandson. Langston, who was lonely, needed love. He often wished for his mother to come and take him away. She made rare appearances, but always returned him to his grandmother. Langston remembered going to Kansas City with his mother and hearing the blues for the very first time. He and his mother also shared a love for the theater. Langston particularly enjoyed seeing the stage version of *Uncle Tom's Cabin.*

"I was unhappy for a long time, and very lonesome, living with my grandmother. Then it was that books began to happen to me, and I began to believe in nothing but books and the wonderful world in books—where if people suffered they suffered in beautiful language, not in monosyllables, as we did in Kansas,"[10] Langston later wrote.

School gave Langston a place to feel good about himself. He entered second grade at the segregated Pinckney School.

By fifth grade, he was attending the integrated New York School on New York Street, also in Lawrence. At New York School, he was an excellent and well-behaved student. When Langston began junior high at Central School, one of his teachers wanted to seat African American students in one row and white students in the other rows. Langston was infuriated. The practice of segregating African Americans from whites in public places was referred to as "Jim Crow." It wasn't something his grandmother would put up with, and neither did he. He printed cards saying "Jim Crow Row" and chanted the same words at recess. He was expelled from school. The administration was quite unprepared when parents and the community sided with Langston, protesting the idea of a "Jim Crow Row." Langston was readmitted to school, and there was no more talk about segregated seating.

Langston loved school, particularly reading. Besides *Uncle Tom's Cabin*, he enjoyed novels like *The Adventures of Huckleberry Finn* by Mark Twain. He also admired W.E.B. DuBois, author of *The Souls of Black Folk*.

When Langston turned twelve, he had his first paying job. He collected and sold maple seeds to the Bartheldes Seed Company. He also delivered the *Saturday Evening Post* and a local weekly newspaper.

Not long after Langston's thirteenth birthday, his always healthy grandmother fell ill. She died early in the morning on April 8, at age seventy-nine. Langston later recalled, "Somebody woke me up at three o'clock in the morning because my grandmother was dead. I went outdoors looking for my grandmother. She wasn't there. The moon was there, cold and ugly, but no ghost of my Grandmother."[11] After a funeral held in her home, she was buried at Oak Hill Cemetery next to her husband, Charles. The woman who had always been there for Langston was gone.

John Brown and Harpers Ferry

Slavery started in the United States soon after the first Europeans crossed the Atlantic Ocean to settle in the "New World." Some Americans, including the Quakers of Pennsylvania, opposed this institution. Even before the American Revolutionary War, the right or wrong of slavery—and treating people as property—was being debated. People who fought against slavery were called abolitionists. They spoke out against it and even smuggled slaves to "free" states using the Underground Railroad. Soon, attitudes about slavery became largely geographical. People from the North generally opposed slavery, while Southerners generally supported it.

An abolitionist named John Brown dedicated his life to stopping slavery. As a young boy, he helped fugitive slaves escape to Canada. The adult Brown believed in using violence to stop slavery. He and five of his sons moved to

John Brown

Kansas, where people were debating whether the territory would become a free state or a slave state. In 1856, proslavery people killed several abolitionists in Lawrence, Kansas. Brown and his sons avenged their deaths by killing five of the proslavery people.

The incident in Kansas made John Brown infamous, and in some states, a wanted man. Brown wanted to create a safe place for former slaves in the Blue Ridge Mountains of Virginia and Maryland. This would also be a base from which Brown could fight slave owners. First, he'd need weapons. He decided that the best place to get the weapons was at the Harpers Ferry Armory and Arsenal.

Harpers Ferry is a small town in Virginia, only 55 miles northwest of Washington, D.C., where the Potomac and Shenandoah Rivers meet. It was named after Robert Harper, who ran a ferry for people to cross the Potomac River. After the Revolutionary War, the federal government decided the country needed to make its own weapons in case of another war. President George Washington, who had visited Harpers Ferry, decided the town was an ideal location for a federal armory and arsenal. Water was one of the most efficient power sources used in manufacturing at the time. Harpers Ferry had the combined strength of two rivers. By 1805, the Harpers Ferry Arsenal was manufacturing muskets, rifles, and pistols. What government officials didn't realize was that Harpers Ferry would provide one of the factors leading to a civil war.

On October 16, 1859, Brown and his men walked all night in heavy rain to reach Harpers Ferry. After cutting the telegraph wires, the twenty-one-man "army of liberation" captured the federal armory, with plans to take the estimated 100,000 weapons. After three days, they had barricaded themselves in the one-story fire engine and guardhouse as the military from surrounding states, commanded by Colonel (later General) Robert E. Lee, arrived. Seventeen men died in battle; ten were from Brown's group, including two of his sons. Another man who died was Sheridan Leary, Mary Langston's first husband, and one of five African Americans with Brown. On the morning of October 18, twelve U.S. Marines broke down the door of the armory's fire engine house and arrested a wounded Brown and the other survivors.

John Brown was charged and convicted for "conspiring with slaves to commit treason and murder." At his trial in nearby Charlestown, he was sentenced to hang on December 2. Before he died, he said:

> *I wish to say furthermore, that you had better—all you people at the South—prepare yourselves for a settlement of that question that must come up for settlement sooner than you are prepared for it. The sooner you are prepared the better. You may dispose of me very easily; I am nearly disposed of now; but this question is still to be settled—this negro question I mean—the end of that is not yet.*[12]

John Brown became a folk hero to many, who saw him as martyr to end slavery. Eighteen months after his death, the Civil War between North and South began. Harpers Ferry figured prominently in the war, changing hands frequently. The only armory building to survive the war was the fire engine and guardhouse where John Brown and his men had made their last stand. A few years later, Harpers Ferry became the site of Storer College, created for the purpose of educating former slaves. The college closed its doors in 1955. Today, the site of the Harpers Ferry uprising is a National Historic Park, where park rangers lead programs about the important events of John Brown's raid on Harpers Ferry.

Mary Sampson Patterson Leary Langston was Langston's grandmother, with whom he often lived. She was the most stable influence he had as a child and instilled a feeling in him of pride in his ancestors. When she died in 1914, Langston thought he'd be able to live with his mother again.

Chapter 3

Northern Migration

Carrie arrived in Lawrence to attend her mother's funeral with her new husband, Homer Clark, and her two-year-old stepson, Gwyn. Langston was thrilled to finally have a little brother and quickly took to the young boy, whom they all called Kit. After attending the funeral of Mary Langston, it looked as if Langston might finally be getting the family he had always wanted—but then Homer Clark left town. A former cook from Topeka, Clark decided to look for work in Chicago. Although Langston liked his new stepfather and even called him Dad, leaving his family to look for work was a pattern reminiscent of his own mother. Carrie and Kit soon followed Clark to Illinois. It is not clear why, but Langston did not go with them.

Did Langston feel hurt that his new family left him in Lawrence so soon after his grandmother's death? He was only thirteen years old. He doesn't say much about his feelings in his autobiographies. Those who knew Langston best believed he never shared his deepest feelings in his autobiographies. Better clues about his feelings regarding his childhood are found in his poetry and in his novel, *Not Without Laughter*. Biographer Rampersad wrote of Langston, "In some respects, he grew up a motherless and a fatherless child, who never forgot the hurts of his childhood."[1]

Langston stayed in Lawrence with family friends, the Reeds. He and his grandmother had stayed with them many times when Mary Langston had rented out her home. Langston liked James and Mary Reed, who lavished love and attention on the boy. He wrote in *The Big Sea*, ". . . there have never been

23

any better people in the world. I loved them very much."[2] The childless Auntie and Uncle Reed owned their home, which included a small farm. Langston did chores, from taking the cows to pasture to helping with the garden. After years of living with little money to buy food, now he had as much to eat as he wanted. The only thing Auntie Reed asked of him was that he accompany her on Sundays to St. Luke's African Methodist Episcopal Church two blocks away. She was a very religious woman who believed God would take care of Langston. The boy, however, was uncomfortable at church; this was a feeling he would carry with him throughout his life. When he attended a revival with Auntie Reed, he watched as children all around him were converted. Standing alone, with her hopeful eyes upon him, Langston stepped forward, pretending to also be converted. He felt overwhelming guilt and cried himself to sleep that night.

Langston started what he thought of as his first real job at a hotel for white guests. After school each day, he cleaned brass spittoons, mirrors, toilets, halls, and the lobby. It was a job his grandmother would have felt was beneath him, but Langston enjoyed earning fifty cents a week. He used his earnings to go to the theater and watch silent actors like Charlie Chaplin on the movie screen. One day, the movie theater put up a sign that said No Colored Allowed. Signs refusing service to African Americans were going up all over Lawrence. Langston began watching live theater at the Bowersock Opera House instead. Although also owned by whites, the Bowersock allowed African Americans to sit in a separate section. Langston sat in the gallery, often by himself, and watched plays and shows. He also attended nearby college football games on Saturday afternoons, where he rooted for the hometown University of Kansas Jay Hawks.

Although the Reeds gave Langston a sense of security and family that had been missing in his earlier years, he felt like a child no one wanted. He carried this feeling with him throughout his life, as his mother's interest in him ranged from nothing to a strong financial and emotional dependence upon him. Even so, he was lonely for his mother. He later remembered, "When I went to live with Auntie Reed, whose house was near the depot, I used to walk down to the Santa Fe station and stare at the railroad tracks, because the railroad tracks ran to Chicago, and Chicago was the biggest town in the world to me, much talked of by the people in Kansas."[3] It was also where his mother was.

By the summer of 1918, Langston's mother had him join them in Lincoln, Illinois. Not far from Chicago, Lincoln was the first town in the United States named after Abraham Lincoln. Biographer Rampersad wrote that the town of

12,000 would be significant in another way too: He would write his first poetry there.

As before, Langston was a brilliant student who got along well with others at Lincoln's Central School. He and one girl were the only African Americans in his eighth-grade class. Interestingly, it was perhaps because he was African American that he was introduced to poetry. His classmates chose him as class poet. Langston said, "In America most white people think, of course, that *all* Negroes can sing and dance, and have a sense of rhythm. So my classmates, knowing that a poem had to have rhythm, elected me unanimously—thinking, no doubt, that I had some, being a Negro. It never occurred to me to be a poet before, or indeed a writer of any kind."[4]

The only poems Langston remembered liking as a child were the African American dialect poems by Paul Lawrence Dunbar. Dunbar was one of the earliest African American poets to use the exaggerated accents and colorful expressions of dialects. Langston also liked *Hiawatha* by Henry Wadsworth Longfellow. He preferred reading novels and read anything his mother brought home from the public library. His favorite authors included Edna Ferber and western writer Zane Grey. *Riders of the Purple Sage* was a favorite book.

Langston began the class poem with verses in appreciation of the school's eight teachers. The second half referred to how great their eighth-grade graduating class of eighty students was. Langston read the poem at the graduation and received much applause. His stepfather missed the graduation; Clark had left again. Soon after graduation, Langston and the rest of the family joined Clark in Cleveland, Ohio.

World War I had started and the Industrial Revolution was going strong. The change in industry marked a huge migration of African Americans from the South to the North, where more jobs were available. From 1910 to 1920, the African American population of Cleveland doubled. Homer Clark found a decent paying job in a steel mill. When he could no longer stand the heat of the furnaces, he got a job as a building caretaker, and later as a janitor. Rents were high, even for their basement apartment, so Carrie began working as a maid.

Cleveland was the eighth city he had lived in, but Langston loved it. According to Rampersad, "For Hughes, his arrival marked the first satisfaction of what would be his lifelong passion for cities; the older he became, the less tolerant he grew of the country."[5]

Central High School in Cleveland was founded in 1846, making it the oldest high school in Ohio. It became significant to Langston as the only high school he would attend. Although his mother and stepfather continued to move around, Langston was determined to finish his education at Central. The school enjoyed a good reputation as one of the best public schools. It had turned out successful graduates, including millionaire John D. Rockefeller. Yet by the time Langston enrolled in school, white Americans were moving away from the inner city and being replaced with recent immigrants. Many students at Central were the children of parents born in countries like Hungary, Italy, or Russia. His best friend's family came from Poland. Langston and the fair-haired Sartur Andrzejewski remained friends throughout the four years.

As usual, Langston was one of few African Americans attending the school. With his likable personality, he was popular with students and teachers. During his freshman year, he studied graphic arts and thought he might be a draftsman someday. After school, he worked in Mrs. Kitzmiller's store, selling ice cream and watermelon to people who arrived daily from the South. He worked in a department store during the summer. He watched in amazement as people spent what would amount to six months' rent for his family just for one gold cigarette lighter.

Langston started his sophomore year at Central only to see Clark leave the family for Chicago again. When his mother and Kit followed, Langston took an attic room and lived on his own. He was determined to continue his schooling. He ate a lot of hot dogs and white rice because these were the only things he knew how to cook. Sometimes his friend's family, the Andrzejewskis, took pity on him and invited him over for a Polish dinner of cabbage.

Langston also met Russell and Rowena Jelliffe, a young white couple dedicated to community service work in Cleveland. They established the first African American theater, Karamu House, around the corner from Langston's first Cleveland home. He liked that their purpose was to promote interracial harmony. Langston was one of the first children to attend the community center, where he took art classes. Soon, he was teaching art to children at the "Playground House." For Langston, the Jelliffes became his home away from home. He began spending more time at their house, where he could relax.

An honor student, Langston joined the track team during his sophomore year. He also began submitting poetry to the school's monthly magazine, the *Belfry Owl*. His first serious effort, "The Red Cross Nurse," was a popular choice during wartime. He soon began publishing regularly in the magazine. Even more importantly, his English teacher, Ethel Weimer, introduced him to the works of what would be his greatest influences, Carl Sandburg and Walt Whitman.

Whitman helped him understand the self-respect that the common man possessed. Langston called Sandburg his guiding star and even wrote a poem dedicated to him. In *The Big Sea,* he would explain: "Little Negro dialect poems like Paul Lawrence Dunbar's and poems without rhyme like Sandburg's were the first real poems I tried to write."[6]

With his life going fairly well in Cleveland, Langston visited his family that summer in Chicago. It was an uncomfortable summer in their crowded room, which was located near the elevated railway known as the El. Clark had taken off again, and Carrie was working for a hat maker. She got Langston a job delivering the hats. Most of Langston's deliveries were in white neighborhoods. One day a gang of white boys beat him up. When it was time to return to school, his mother wanted him to remain in Chicago. Unlike her own parents, Carrie Clark felt that her son would be more useful if he quit school and got a job. "My mother, as a great many poor mothers do, seemed to have the fixed idea that a son is born for the sole purpose of taking care of his parents as soon as possible,"[7] Langston explained. Living alone during his sophomore year had given Langston the confidence to refuse his mother. He knew the importance of an education, even if she didn't. He happily left Chicago for Cleveland to begin his junior year.

At the beginning of the school year, Langston joined the staff of the *Belfry Owl.* He continued writing poetry and also wrote some short stories. His first short story, titled "Those Who Have No Turkey," was published in the school paper in December. It is the story of fifteen-year-old Diane Jordan, visiting her well-off aunt in the city for Thanksgiving. When she meets a newsboy whose family is too poor to buy a turkey, she invites him and his family to her aunt's. After Christmas, students saw Langston's name often in *The Belfry Owl.* The school's literary magazine published many of his poems. In his first autobiography, Langston wrote that it was during the 1918–1919 school year that he first began thinking about being a writer.

Langston stayed busy during the school year. Perhaps it helped ward off the loneliness he felt as a sixteen-year-old boy living alone. He was proud of his achievements in track, lettering in the high jump and the 440 relay. He was also active in the student council, French Club, and American Civic Association. According to Langston, most of the students in his school were either Catholic or Jewish. Because neither group wanted to vote for the other, Langston held many class offices as a compromise between the Catholic and Jewish students of the school.

His first date was attending the symphony with a Jewish girl. Although his best friend was Catholic, he found it easier to get to know the Jewish students, many of whose families came from Eastern Europe. Langston and his fellow students heard about the Russian Revolution of 1917 when the Russian people overthrew the czarist government and installed a socialist government. Langston began reading borrowed socialist magazines like the *Liberator*. The more Langston heard about this theory of government, which emphasized collective ownership, the more he suspected that socialist governments were less racist toward African Americans.

Although he was generally happy at Central High School, problems did come up. His high school class went on a field trip to hear opera legend Sara Bernhardt sing. Afterward, they went across the street to eat at the cafeteria. The cashier rang up Sartur's food, which amounted to forty-five or fifty cents. When it was Langston's turn, he said she took one look at this face and then kept hitting the cash register keys. Although he had the same food as Sartur, his bill came to $8.65. When he asked why it was so high, the cashier told him that that was how much it would cost him to eat at the cafeteria. An upset Langston left. He later called the incident "my most humiliating Jim Crow experience."[8]

Langston's mother and stepbrother returned to Cleveland. Clark also returned briefly. Langston's biggest surprise came late in the school year when he received a letter from his father. It was short and to the point. James Hughes wrote to say that he was coming to take Langston to Mexico for the summer. Carrie was furious and didn't want Langston to go. "I said I wanted to go to Mexico for the summer to see what the country was like—and my father. Then I would be back in the fall," he wrote.[9]

Langston's mind was full of the man he hadn't seen for eleven years. His only memory of his father was his strong arms cradling Langston as he carried him out of the hotel in Mexico City during the earthquake that had sent Carrie fleeing back to the United States. Langston looked forward to meeting his father again. Maybe he would finally feel like he belonged somewhere.

His mother refused to see him off. Furthermore, she wouldn't write to him during the entire summer. Through a mixup, he was late in meeting his father at the train station. James Hughes only questioned where he had been. Although it had been eleven years, Langston noticed that his father never said he was glad to see him. The long train ride gave the young man plenty of time to get to know his father. It is likely that Langston realized what an unlikable person his father was before they ever arrived in Mexico.

28

James Hughes was a small, angry man whose only goal in life seemed to be to gain wealth. When he left the United States to explore opportunities in Spanish-speaking countries, he tried various things, including practicing law in Mexico. When the Mexican Revolution of 1910 started, many white Americans fled the country. Their departure opened more opportunities for Hughes. By the time of Langston's visit, his father was managing an electric light company and had acquired a ranch and rental property in Mexico City. He was doing quite well, but it seemed the more money he earned, the less he liked parting with it. It had been one of the things he had fought about with his wife. Carrie enjoyed money too, but she wanted to spend it.

Almost as strong as James Hughes's desire for money was his hatred of poor nonwhite people. He admired the growing German community in Mexico, but spoke contemptuously about African Americans and Mexicans. "My father hated Negroes. I think he hated himself, too, for being a Negro," Langston revealed. "He disliked all of his family because they were Negroes and remained in the United States."[10]

Langston and his father got off the train in Mexico City. They stayed briefly at the Grand Hotel and checked on his properties, managed by the three Patiño sisters, Cuca, Fela, and Lola. The three women seemed to be the only people who truly liked James Hughes.

Mexico was known for its bullfights, and Langston had been looking forward to seeing one himself. However, his father was in a hurry to return home to Toluca. They boarded another train for the short trip west of Mexico City. The train wound through the mountains, climbing higher and higher to reach Toluca, located in a green valley with lakes and a view of the snow-capped volcano known as La Nevada de Toluca.

They disembarked at the Toluca train station and walked the short distance to Hughes's home. A high adobe wall surrounded the house and a corral that held horses and chickens. Instead of showing his son the sights of central Mexico, Hughes quickly put Langston to work learning bookkeeping. Langston told his father that he wasn't much good at math, which infuriated James. He yelled at Langston for not having a good head for business. As Langston soon learned, his father frequently yelled. He often yelled at his son and his two servants to "hurry up." James Hughes was always in a hurry, and he expected those around him to hurry also.

His father often worked away from home. Langston spent free time with Maximiliano, an Indian boy who was his father's servant. After Maximiliano taught Langston how to handle a horse, Langston would ride a black horse named Tito to nearby villages. Hughes's other servant was a cook who was limited to making the same beef and beans each day. Hughes refused to spend extra money for food. When his father went out of town on business, Langston ordered lots of good food from the local shops. He told the storekeepers to put it on his father's bill. When he returned, James Hughes was very angry. He berated his son and told him he was just like his mother. Regardless, the household ate well while the food lasted. James Hughes was not about to waste food.

Langston learned to speak and read Spanish in his free time. His knowledge of Spanish helped when he attended the Sunday movies in the village. Most of the time, he was bored and unhappy. He sank into a depression. His father was not the man he had hoped he would be.

Langston fell ill in August. His stomach hurt, and he couldn't eat. He also ran a high fever. When he didn't get any better, the local doctor recommended that he be admitted to the hospital. Hughes took Langston to the American Hospital in Mexico City, where he was diagnosed with a stomach infection. Langston had a different diagnosis: "But I never told them or the doctors that I was sick because I hated my father."[11]

It took several weeks for Langston to recover. When he found out it was costing his stingy father twenty dollars a day for the hospital, Langston took his time getting better. As soon as he was well enough, he boarded the train to Cleveland. "That summer in Mexico was the most miserable I have ever known," he wrote. "I did not hear from my mother for several weeks. I did not like my father. And I did not know what to do about either of them."[12]

World War I ended just before Langston returned to America. Although the battles overseas had ended, new fighting was just beginning in America as racially charged riots broke out in many cities. As had happened in Lawrence, Cleveland businesses began refusing to admit African Americans. African Americans were fired from jobs that were then given to the white soldiers returning home.

Langston helped his mother make ends meet by working in a dining room in a Cleveland hotel. She was still angry with him for visiting his father. She told him she was looking forward to this being Langston's last year of high school, because she expected him to start working right after graduation and be of some use to her. No doubt Langston stayed away from home as much as possible. He became a frequent visitor to the Cleveland Public Library. The children's services director, Effie Power, encouraged the young student. Her encouragement meant a lot to him. Years later, she asked Hughes for a selection of his poems suitable for children. *The Dream Keeper* was published with an introduction by the librarian.

No matter how unhappy Langston's home life was, he still shined at school. He continued to stand out in track and many organizations. He was chosen as the yearbook editor and even acted in some high school plays at the encouragement of Sartur. Many students liked the handsome, athletic, friendly young man. Not surprisingly, Langston was elected class poet. He was writing more and more and had a notebook full of poems, including "When Sue Wears Red" about a girl he met at a dance. This was the first time he had written a poem about a girl in whom he was interested. The poem celebrated African American beauty and would later be published in *The Crisis*. It began:

> *When Susanna Jones wears red*
> *Her face is like an ancient cameo*
> *Turned brown by the ages.*[13]

Langston graduated from high school with honors in June. He wanted to go to college but didn't have the money. His mother continued to insist that he didn't need to go to college. She wanted him to help pay the bills with a job. Her lack of support must have been painful. Years later, he wrote a heart-wrenching one-act play called *Soul Gone Home*. In the play, the mother berates her son for not helping her by getting a job.

When James Hughes wrote his son about coming to Mexico to discuss his future, Langston was interested. The memory of the previous disastrous summer was still strong, but Hughes hinted that he might send Langston to college. Since Langston wanted to go to college more than anything else, he left for Mexico to see what his father was willing to do for his future.

The Influences of Sandburg and Whitman

Walt Whitman (1819–1892) and Carl Sandburg (1878–1967) shared many characteristics with each other. Both left school at an early age. As the second oldest in his family, Whitman was helping to support his large family from the time he was eleven. Within a year, he became a printer's apprentice and fell in love with the written word. He began reading any book he could get his hands on, including works by Homer, Dante, and Shakespeare. Sandburg left school at thirteen, but continued his education by hopping on trains and seeing the

Walt Whitman

country. Years later, his love of America was reflected in his poetry. Yet Sandburg also was realistic. His poem "Chicago" focused on the brutality and ugliness of cities. Whitman was a lifelong New Yorker, who, like Langston Hughes, preferred America's cities, particularly the people and culture of New York City.

War strongly affected both poets. Sandburg, who was born fourteen years after the Civil War, would fight in the Spanish-American War. His experience convinced him that war should be avoided whenever possible. Even so, he discovered his hero in the events of the Civil War, fellow Illinoisian Abraham Lincoln. Sandburg's admiration of Lincoln motivated him to write a well-researched multivolume work on Abraham Lincoln and the Civil War, which brought him his first Pulitzer Prize—for history, in 1940. He later won a Pulitzer Prize for Poetry.

Whitman spent the Civil War working unofficially as a nurse in the military hospitals after visiting a wounded brother at Fredericksburg. Hughes later wrote about Whitman: "He hated war and killing, but he devoted much of his time to nursing and caring for the wounded, both Northern and Southern, white or Negro, Yankee or Rebel."[14]

Like the rest of the country, Whitman was shocked by the assassination of President Lincoln in 1865. He wrote "O Captain! My Captain!" about Lincoln.

> O Captain! my Captain! rise up and hear the bells;
> Rise up—for you the flag is flung—for you the bugle trills; For you
> bouquets and ribbon'd wreaths—for you the shores a-crowding;
> For you they call, the swaying mass, their eager faces turning;
> Here Captain! dear father!
> This arm beneath your head;
> It is some dream that on the deck,
> You've fallen cold and dead.[15]

Whitman had already self-published a twelve-poem collection called *Leaves of Grass* in 1851. No publisher would touch the book. After Whitman's death, *Leaves of Grass* would become acknowledged as one of the greatest works of poetry in the world, particularly the fifty-two-stanza "Song of Myself." Whitman's style, known as "thought rhythm," had more in common with the writing found in the Bible's Old Testament than the English Romantic poetry of the period. Sandburg, who was often compared to Whitman, took poetry form and style further. His free-style poetry was often criticized as being too sentimental.

Both Whitman and Sandburg broke down the walls of what was considered poetry. Langston Hughes would later do the same. Hughes and Sandburg probably crossed paths on occasion. Both received honorary doctorates from Lincoln University in 1943.

Walt Whitman had a continued impact on Hughes. One of Hughes's greatest honors occurred after his second volume of poetry, *Fine Clothes to the Jew,* was published. The Walt Whitman Foundation invited Hughes to read his poems at the Walt Whitman Camden House in New Jersey. Hughes told the audience that his own verse came from the example set by Whitman. In 1946, Hughes edited *I Hear the People Singing: Selected Poems of Walt Whitman.* And in 1953, he wrote a column in *The Chicago Defender,* "Whitman: Negroes' First Great Poetic Friend."

Langston Hughes by Winold Reiss, 1925, shows the poet sitting in thought. It was during this time period that Hughes first gained recognition as a poet after winning a poetry prize sponsored by *Opportunity* magazine.

Chapter 4

"I've Known Rivers"

Langston went to the train station alone again; his mother refused to come with him to see him off. For this trip to Mexico, he traveled alone. He felt guilty about going against his mother's wishes and was probably nervous about seeing his father again too. He did what he often did at times like this: He wrote. "For my best poems were all written when I felt the worst," he claimed. "When I was happy, I didn't write anything."[1]

One day at sunset, the train traveled across a long bridge over the Mississippi River. The sight of the sun setting on the river led him to thinking about the history of the river, particularly for African Americans. He considered the many rivers that are important in the history of the African people: Euphrates, Nile, Mississippi. He began writing on the back of an envelope. After ten or fifteen minutes, he had written a poem that would someday be printed again and again. It was called "The Negro Speaks of Rivers," and it began like this:

I've known rivers:
I've known rivers ancient as the world and older than the flow
of human blood in human veins

My soul has grown deep like the rivers.[2]

When Langston arrived in Mexico, he found that his father had hired a German housekeeper, Berta Schultz. His father often spoke German at home and

Spanish at work, rarely any English. As before, James Hughes worked most of the time. Langston found himself with nothing much to do. He became acquainted with Schultz, a widow with a young daughter. Schultz would wed his father in 1924 and stay married to him for a brief period of time. Langston improved his Spanish until he was more comfortable going out and talking to other people. He borrowed books from the library, reading novels in Spanish by authors such as Blasco Ibáñez, who wrote *The Four Horsemen of the Apocalypse*. And Langston wrote. He penned descriptions of life in Mexico. He completed his first one-act play, *The Gold Piece*. And he wrote poems. *Aunt Sue's Stories* was a tribute to the women who raised him, his grandmother and Auntie Reed. When Langston wrote *Mother to Son*, he described a woman whose life had been difficult, but she kept on climbing.

Langston waited for his father to bring up the subject of college and his future, as his letter had hinted. The opportunity came later that summer as they traveled to his father's ranch with German mining investors. It was a difficult trip, riding horses over mountains and rocky trails while staying alert to possible bandits waiting to rob travelers. They talked little as they concentrated on riding. At one point James grumbled about the leaders in the Mexican Revolution, a fight for independence that had been ongoing since 1910. He called men like Emiliano Zapata and Pancho Villa bandits. Langston admired the revolutionaries and disagreed with his father. He said the two men just wanted to get the land back for the peasants.

They arrived at Hughes's ranch as the sun was going down. The next day, they took the Germans to a flooded mine shaft nearby. James Hughes believed that the silver mines would be very productive within five or six years. He mentioned that this was enough time for Langston to study mining engineering in Switzerland or Germany, and then return to Mexico to work for his father.

Langston was shocked. It had never occurred to him to study mining engineering or to go to school in Europe. Besides, math had continued to be his worst subject. Hughes related the tense conversation in his autobiography. His father asked him, "What do you want to be?"

"I don't know. But I think a writer."
"A writer?" my father said. "A writer? Do they make any money?"[3]

Nothing had changed. Money was still very important to James Hughes, and he couldn't understand why it wasn't important to his son. He said that no

African American could get ahead by going to college in the United States. He told his son that he would pay for his education only if he studied mining engineering in Europe. Langston refused. He wanted to study writing at Columbia University in New York, also the doorway to the African American community of Harlem.

September came, and college started. Hughes decided to stay in Mexico for the remainder of the school year and make his own money. His father wouldn't pay for college or the train trip back to the United States. Langston began teaching English and was soon in very high demand. Mornings were spent teaching women in a private school, and he taught at a business college most afternoons. He also taught private students from prominent families in town. He didn't save much money. He was sending some of his earnings to his mother in Cleveland.

In his free time, Langston attended bullfights in Mexico City. He became a huge fan, even participating with the locals as they dove into the ring afterward for souvenir banderillas, the ornamental darts set in the bull. For years, Langston prized a pair of burnt orange banderillas with tinseled gold that he had grabbed. When he won them, the bull's hair and blood still covered them. Langston wanted very much to write about bullfights—the sights, sounds, and smells. "I tried to write about a bullfight, but could never capture it on paper," he admitted. "Bullfights are very hard things to put down on paper—like trying to describe the ballet."[4]

Langston began sending some of his writing to magazines for publication. For children, he wrote stories about life and the games played in Mexico. *Brownies' Book*, a children's magazine published by the NAACP, printed his work in five issues. He wrote about Toluca in the articles "In a Mexican City" and "Up to the Crater of an Old Volcano." He also sold his play, *The Gold Piece: A Play That Might Be True*. Editor Jessie Fauset encouraged him to send more.

Before New Year's Day in 1921, Langston took a chance and sent her the poem from his train ride, "The Negro Speaks of Rivers." Fauset loved it and placed it in the adult NAACP publication, *The Crisis*. The executive editor was one of his heroes, W.E.B. DuBois. During Langston's time in Mexico, his poetry, short stories, essays, and drama continued to appear in the two U.S. publications. "Neither the *Crisis* nor the *Brownies' Book* paid anything, but I was delighted to be published," he later wrote. "For the next few years my poems appeared often (and solely) in the *Crisis*. And to that magazine, certainly, I owe my literary beginnings."[5]

The Crisis has been the official monthly publication of the NAACP since 1910. With W.E.B. DuBois as the first editor, it soon became the leading magazine for African Americans. In addition to speaking out against lynching and discrimination, *The Crisis* published leading African American writers and artists. When Hughes began contributing to *The Crisis*, it sold for tens cents a copy and boasted a monthly circulation of 80,000. For fifteen cents, children could read news, poems, and short fiction in *The Brownies' Book,* which was published for two years. Jessie Fauset was editor of *The Brownies' Book* and literary editor for *The Crisis.*

James Hughes noticed his son's published work and finally agreed to pay for a year at Columbia. If he did well, his father would pay for further college. Langston had spent over a year in Mexico—a long time for a young man who would believe that six months in one place complicated his life. He said good-bye to his father in Mexico City and took a train to the Gulf coast port of Veracruz, where he boarded a ship for New York. Langston would never see his father again.

Hughes could barely contain his excitement as he arrived in New York City. He later recalled his first glimpse. "New York was pretty, rising out of the bay in the sunset—the thrill of those towers of Manhattan with their million golden eyes, growing slowly taller and taller above the green water, until they looked as if they could almost touch the sky! Then Brooklyn Bridge, gigantic in the dusk! Then the necklaces of lights, glowing everywhere around us, as we docked on the Brooklyn side. All this made me feel it was better to come to New York than to any other city in the world."[6]

In contrast, Columbia University was a cold, imposing campus that left Hughes with a strong desire to be elsewhere. His father had already paid his tuition, so he checked in at Hartley Hall dormitory. The clerk took one look at him and told him there were no rooms left. Hughes showed her his reservation. Because the reservation came from Toluca, Mexico, the school had been uncertain of his race. To Hughes, it was evident that they were sorry he wasn't Mexican. Since a deposit had already been paid, there wasn't much to be done but give him a room.

Most of the schools Hughes had attended in his short life had student populations that were mainly white. He was used to being one of only a few African American students. This hadn't stopped his popularity with students from all races. Columbia was different. No one nominated him for class offices or encouraged him to try out for plays. At first, he tried to fit in. When he joined the school newspaper, *The Spectator,* he was assigned to cover white-only society news and fraternities. He quit. The only student Hughes got to know was Chun, a young man from China.

Yet as much as he didn't fit in at Columbia, he did fit in in Harlem. Harlem stretched north from 130th to 145th Street, and from Fifth to Eighth Avenue. Originally started as a Dutch village, Harlem was becoming increasingly populated with African Americans from the southern United States and the West Indies. The southern edge of Harlem bordering Central Park was largely populated by whites, but the neighborhood was being called the "Negro capital of the world." Hughes's first trip on a subway train, the Lenox Avenue subway, took him to 135th Street. He immediately felt at home. "Harlem! I stood there, dropped my bags, took a deep breath and felt happy again!"[7]

When Jessie Fauset learned that one of her most talented young writers was now living in New York, she invited him to the *Crisis* offices on Fifth Avenue in Greenwich Village. The idea of meeting W.E.B. DuBois terrified Hughes. Not only had his grandmother read DuBois to him as a child, but *Souls of Black Folks* was the first book Hughes had read on his own. As the first African American man to receive a doctoral degree from Harvard, DuBois's middle-class life was very different from Hughes's upbringing. Hughes invited his mother, now living in New York, to go with him to the *Crisis* office and later to lunch at the Civic Club. If nothing else, Carrie Clark was comfortable socially with other people.

Hughes needn't have worried. The legendary DuBois reportedly enjoyed meeting the young poet, who would have been about the same age as DuBois's son had he lived. Langston immediately took to Jessie Fauset, and soon they were discussing plays and movies they could write together.

Hughes hated his classes at Columbia, and he hated having to account to his father for every cent he spent. His rather meager allowance was stretched even further because he was supporting his mother and stepbrother. He borrowed many of his textbooks from the library. The winter was cold, and he had no money for winter clothing. Education had always been important to Hughes, but he could hardly stand to be at Columbia. Instead, he began spending more and more time in Harlem. He listened to lectures and readings at the Harlem Branch of the New York Public Library. It was there that he discovered the Schomburg Collection of Negro Literature and History. He saw most of the major Broadway productions, including the first Broadway musical with an all–African American cast, *Shuffle Along*. Hughes might be listening to the blues at the Lincoln Theater one night and attending plays the next night at the La-fayette. A *Crisis* staff member arranged for him to give his first reading at the

Harlem Community Church. At the time, public readings paid nothing, but they would later when Hughes spent several months a year reading his poetry at churches, schools, libraries, and community centers.

He had few surprises at the end of the school year. He had done fairly well in English and French, but poorly in physics and trigonometry. And although he had lettered in high school track, he flunked a college physical education class. It didn't matter to Hughes, who had already decided that he wasn't going back to Columbia. He wrote to his father, telling him that he was quitting college and getting a job. Hughes received a letter from one of his father's colleagues reporting that his father had suffered a stroke and wanted Langston to come to Mexico. A hundred dollars was included. Before reaching a decision, he received word that his father was improving except for a paralyzed right arm. Hughes declined to visit, saying that his relationship with his father was so tense that he couldn't possibly do his father any good. He returned the $100, but guilt forced him to write to his father a few times. When he received no reply, Hughes finally stopped writing.

His mother was again living with Homer Clark. At twenty years old, Hughes felt ready to start his own life. He rented a room in Harlem and began applying for jobs. Again and again, he was turned down because he wasn't white. He was finally hired at a Staten Island farm for the summer. He earned $50 a month plus food and a place to sleep, which was on a haystack. Hughes worked long hours every day and enjoyed it. He felt like one of the common men Whitman had written about.

When summer ended, so did the job. Hughes delivered flowers for just one month before getting fired for being late. He decided that if he was only going to get such low pay anyway, he might as well see the world while he was at it. He began hanging around the docks, looking for a job as a mess boy. Many of the ships had all-white crews, but he finally found a job on a freighter called the *West Hassayampa*. Imagine his surprise when the ship didn't sail into the ocean but north up the Hudson River for forty miles. Their destination was a ship graveyard near Jones Point, just south of West Point Military School. The sight of eighty "dead" World War I ships sitting in the Hudson was eerie. Hughes and the crew, made up largely of new immigrants to the United States, would live on the mother ship and maintain the war ships by oiling the machinery and cables. Planks connected all the ships together. The ships were to be maintained in case there was another war.

Hughes was disappointed that the only sight he was going to see was all these ships in the Hudson River. Winter in northern New York isolated the crew even further as snow fell around them. When the river iced up, there was no way to get to shore unless the ice was definitely hard enough to walk on. Hughes didn't seem to mind. The work was easy and left plenty of time for reading and writing. He wrote more than twelve poems in his five months on the ship. Eleven of these would be published in *Crisis*.

One of the ships was rumored to be haunted. It was a shabby-looking boat with dust and cobwebs. Bullet holes decorated the steel bridge where the captain had supposedly been killed. One of Hughes's crewmates, an Irish fireman, bet that nobody would spend a night alone on the boat. As the only African American among the crew, Hughes felt he had something to prove. He later explained his reasons. "They had all seen Negroes in the motion pictures portrayed so often as superstitious and frightened, that I guess that was another reason for my going. I wanted to prove to them Negroes are not more afraid of ghosts than other people."[8]

Hughes went over to the creaking boat one windy night. Men from the crew tried to sneak up to the haunted ship and scare him, but Hughes slept through the night with no trouble. He won a much-needed ten dollars from the bet.

When springtime arrived, Hughes decided to find another job on a ship that was actually going somewhere. He arrived in the New York City shipping office with a good recommendation in his pocket from the *West Hassayampa* captain. He immediately found a job. This ship was definitely going somewhere—Africa.

The NAACP

The Thirteenth Amendment of the United States Constitution abolished slavery in 1865. The Fourteenth Amendment followed, stating that all people born in the United States were citizens. Passed by Congress in 1869, the Fifteenth Amendment stated: "the right of citizens of the United States to vote shall not be denied or abridged by the United States or by any State on account of race, color, or previous condition of servitude."[9] Forty years after these amendments, these free Americans of African ancestry could not live where they wanted. They could not always go to schools in their own neighborhoods. Almost all colleges refused to admit them. The only jobs available were those that white people didn't want—and they were mainly jobs of servitude. Simple things like going to a public restroom or watching a movie were made more difficult by the Jim Crow laws that encouraged segregation between whites and African Americans. Getting a drink of water from the wrong water fountain might lead to a person being arrested or beaten up. Acts of violence by whites toward African Americans were rarely punished and were sometimes even encouraged.

A group of people believed that the treatment of African Americans in the United States was very wrong. Ida Wells-Barnett, W.E.B. DuBois, Henry Moscowitz, Mary White Ovington, Oswald Garrison Villiard, and William English Walling joined together to fight this unfair behavior. On February 12, 1909, they created the National Negro Committee. The name was later changed to The National Association for the Advancement of Colored People, or NAACP. Today, the NAACP is the oldest civil rights organization in the world. For almost a hundred years, it has been one of the most important civil rights groups to fight inequality and discrimination through the legal and judicial systems. Its mission, according to its web site, "is to ensure the political, educational, social and economic equality of rights of all persons and to eliminate racial hatred and racial discrimination."[10]

Although the NAACP supports and encourages creative and educational pursuits, it has been most effective as a political tool. The organization pressured presidents Franklin Roosevelt and Harry S Truman to make discrimination in federal employment illegal, which later led to the passage of the Equal Employment Opportunity Act. The act prohibits discrimination in employment for reasons of race, color, religion, sex, or national origin.

In 1933, the NAACP won the legal battle to admit an African American student to the University of Maryland. Later, it fought segregation in public schools, winning the battle in *Brown vs. the Board of Education of Topeka* in

1954. Thurgood Marshall was the lawyer for the NAACP Legal Defense and Educational Fund that argued these cases before the Supreme Court. Years later, he was appointed by President Lyndon Johnson as the first African American Justice of the U.S. Supreme Court.

African Americans were given the right to vote in the nineteenth century, but places in the South made illegal rules that kept African Americans from voting. The NAACP went to Congress and encouraged the passage of the Civil Rights Act of 1957. After the Voting Rights Act of 1965 was passed, members of the NAACP and other organizations registered more than 80,000 voters in the South.

Meanwhile, when Rosa Parks refused to give up her seat on a bus one fateful day in 1955, and North Carolina students refused to give up seats at whites-only lunch counters, the NAACP supported peaceful protests and pushed for the Civil Rights Act of 1964.

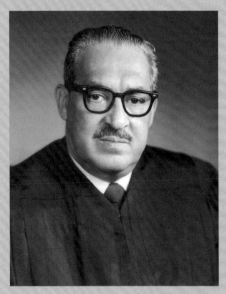

Thurgood Marshall

The NAACP was one of many groups to pressure the United States to impose economic restrictions on South Africa until they ended their system of segregation known as apartheid. Other notable legislation with which the NAACP has been involved includes the creation of the Equal Employment Opportunity Commission and the Fair Housing Act, which was passed in 1968 and expanded in the 1980s. In the 1970s and 1980s, the NAACP made sure the Voting Rights Act was extended.

Because discrimination against African Americans and other minority groups has not been eradicated in the United States, the NAACP is still an active organization. More than 100,000 members continue to work to end discrimination, just as the illustrious members of the past have done. The national office of the NAACP is in Washington, D.C., but members reside all over the world.

Two women walk along a beach in Senegal, located on the west coast of Africa. Senegal was one of the African countries Hughes visited in 1923 when he worked on the ship the *West Hesseltine*.

Chapter

5

Sailing to Africa

Hughes set sail on the *West Hesseltine* on June 13, 1923. His ship carried machinery, tools, canned goods, movies, and missionaries. He was twenty-one and bursting with excitement at the thought of seeing Africa, the land of his ancestors.

One of the things Hughes brought on board was a box of books. After all, books had often kept him company in the past. However, when he opened the box, he was reminded of living in attics, in basements, and in Mexico. Always lonely, he remembered not belonging at Columbia. Perhaps memories of growing up without the emotional support of parents haunted him also. He carried the box of books on deck and looked out over the vast ocean. He picked up each book and threw it into the water. All except one. He kept Walt Whitman's *Leaves of Grass*. It was with this event that he begins his first autobiography, *The Big Sea*. There he commented, "Melodramatic maybe, it seems to me now. But then it was like throwing a million bricks out of my heart when I threw the books into the water."[1]

The freighter had a crew of forty-two. Hughes served three meals a day and tidied the officers' quarters. He did a little writing, but spent most of his free time with the rowdy crew.

When the ship arrived in Africa, Hughes was thrilled at what he saw: "People, black and beautiful as the night,"[2] he later wrote. The *West Hesseltine* and her crew moved down the west coast, stopping at each port to unload cargo and people—and to take away palm oil, ivory, cocoa beans, and mahogany. The

West Hesseltine stopped at more than thirty ports, from the Ivory Coast to the Gold Coast, and from Senegal to Angola. Hughes began to notice that most of the ports were controlled by a European country: Britain, France, Portugal, or Belgium. To his surprise, colonialism was alive and well in Africa, leaving white men in charge. Hughes saw further evidence of similarities to America. Instead of Whites Only signs, businesses hung up Europeans Only signs. In the churches, Africans were required to sit in the back rows while the white missionaries sat in the front rows—just like the Jim Crow row from his school in Kansas.

Hughes tried to tell Africans that he had the same problems as they did. America used Jim Crow laws to treat African Americans as second-class citizens. Africans laughed at Hughes, whom they called a white man. One man explained that Africans called anyone who did not have the darkest skin, white. Hughes shook his head in amazement. No one in America would think the coppery skin color he inherited from his grandmother was anything but a sign that he was African American. Skin color, he was learning, was an issue whether you lived in Africa, the West Indies, or America. It all depended upon a person's interpretation.

Although Hughes was disappointed at the state of affairs in Africa—because they were not so different from those in America—he still tried to make the most of his trip. One night at the Niger River, he watched houseboats in the river, their lanterns swaying with the boat. Giant foreign ships stood attention in the distance. Hughes wrote: "Far off, at the edge of the clearing, over against the forest, I heard the drums of Omali, the JuJu. Above, the moon was like a gold ripe fruit in heaven, too sweet for the taste of man. For a long time I could not sleep."[3]

While in the Congo, many of the crew took the opportunity to buy exotic pets, like parrots and monkeys. Hughes paid three shillings, a shirt, and a pair of shoes for a red monkey. He named it Jocko and planned to give it to his brother, Kit. Jocko often traveled on Hughes's shoulders. It would bite him when he put it down.

He learned a lot on the trip to Africa, both about the country of his ancestors and about himself. He looked forward to returning to America. The ship arrived in New York on an autumn day. Immediately, the crew was fired. According to the paymaster, the crew's behavior had been poor on the return trip.

Hughes didn't mind being jobless again, but he had trouble finding a place to stay with a monkey around his neck. He finally boarded a train for McKeesport, Pennsylvania, where his family was living. He kept Jocko hidden in a bag with holes cut out so that it could breathe. When Hughes let Jocko out of the bag in his mother's home, only Homer Clark laughed. Kit hid and Carrie screamed. Soon after he left, his mother sold the monkey to a pet store.

The Crisis had published many of Hughes's poems while he was away. More people began to recognize the young writer. He gave readings at the Harlem YMCA, where he renewed his friendship with Countee Cullen. The two had met at the Harlem Branch Library, where many young writers of promise spent time. Hughes had written to Cullen of his adventures in Africa. Although both were talented poets of about the same age, they were very different in style. Cullen was a traditional writer who admired English poets like John Keats. There was nothing traditional about Hughes, who drew his inspiration from the world around him. He and Cullen remained friends for a few years, but eventually parted because of their differences. According to Hughes biographer Arnold Rampersad, "Above all, Cullen wished to be seen not as a Negro poet, but as a poet who happened to be Negro—an attitude Hughes found more than a little perverse."[4]

Hughes struggled with what direction to take his life. Returning to college was on his mind a lot. Jessie Fauset encouraged his writing after *The Crisis* dedicated an entire page to his poems in the August issue. Cullen wanted to introduce him to Alain Locke, a professor at Howard University who had expressed interest in meeting Hughes. Unable to decide, Hughes left again after leaving some of his poems with Cullen to be placed at various publications.

He found work on a freighter ship, the *McKeesport,* which he took to be a good sign, as this was the name of the town where his family was living. The ship sailed to Europe with grain and flour from Hoboken, New Jersey. The twenty-day journey over a stormy Atlantic was rough. They arrived in Rotterdam, Denmark, in time for Christmas. A watchman at the dock took Hughes and some of the crew home with him for the holiday. Hughes practiced his high school French with the man's son-in-law, who was from Paris. Hughes had always wanted to visit Paris, where he heard the people were accepting of African Americans. The young man told Hughes stories about his home. When the *McKeesport* returned to America in January, it was across even stormier seas.

After celebrating his twenty-second birthday at Cullen's home, Hughes boarded the *McKeesport* once more for Holland. For the third time, the crossing of the Atlantic was rocky and hazardous. "When we got to Rotterdam, however, I thought maybe there might be a jinx on our ship, so I got off. I had twenty-five dollars coming. I drew it, packed my bags, and caught the night train for Paris. Good-bye, old freight boat!"[5] Hughes wrote.

Already anxious about making decisions in his life probably made the decision to jump ship easier. Leaving for new places would be a pattern he would repeat when he was uncertain about life. It is interesting that he moved so much, since it was his mother's constant moving when he was a child that contributed to his feeling unloved and unwanted.

Hughes arrived in Paris on the night train and exchanged his last seven dollars for francs. After breakfasting on cheap coffee and a croissant, he walked through the falling snow and marveled at the sights he had read about: the Champs Elysées . . . the Louvre. . . . . All too soon, he realized he was hungry again and had no place to stay. He spent his first night at the Right Bank's district on the hill, Montmartre, after a doorman told him that's where many African Americans could be found.

The men he met were mostly soldiers who had remained in Paris after World War I. Other African Americans were entertainers. The French were big fans of jazz. Jobs were hard to get for Americans unless they were entertainers. While searching for a job, Hughes met a Russian dancer named Sonya. They ended up sharing a room at an inexpensive hotel for a few weeks until she left France. After a month of unsuccessful job searching, he wrote to his mother. For the first time in his life, he asked her for a loan. Hughes had always given part of his income to his mother, and he hoped this time she could help him out. She wrote back to say that she had her own problems that included no job, a husband hospitalized with pneumonia, and flooding near their home. She advised her son to quit his gallivanting all over the world and return home.

No matter how hungry he was, Hughes refused to ask his father to send money. He couldn't stand hearing "I told you so."

He thought he had found the perfect job at a nightclub—as a bouncer. It soon became apparent that he would have to stop a lot of fights. Slight of build, Hughes was not a fighter. He quickly quit the job. Later, he began working for an American-owned nightclub called Le Grand Duc as a dishwasher. He later advanced to waiter. Hughes most enjoyed the impromptu jazz sessions that took place when the club closed. He was inspired to write the poem "Jazz Band in a Parisian Cabaret. "

One day, a coworker asked him to deliver a message to a young lady living on Boulevard St. Michel across from Luxembourg Gardens. Hughes had to take a bus to get there, but was delighted when he met three nice young ladies. In particular, he enjoyed meeting Anne Marie Coussey, whom he called Mary and sometimes Nan in his *Big Sea* biography. Anne's parents were African, but she had been raised and educated in London. She spoke with a British accent and had a privileged upbringing. Anne had read his poems in *The Crisis*. They began spending time together. They enjoyed doing a lot of the same things, whether it was going to the theater, dancing at the Moulin Rouge, or visiting the royal residence at Versailles. Soon, they were in love.

Meanwhile in the United States, two of Langston's poems had appeared somewhere besides *The Crisis*. Jessie Fauset had felt that some of his poems were too radical for *The Crisis*. The socialist magazine *The Messenger,* which Hughes had read in high school, published "Grant Park" and the anti-religion poem "Gods."

Hughes was growing as a poet through experimenting. One technique he was using came from music. He wrote poetry verses that sounded like the blues and jazz rhythms he loved so much. As a traditionalist, Fauset didn't care for poems that used this style, such as "Negro Dancers." Neither did Anne.

Hughes and Coussey talked of getting married. The problem was her father wanted her to marry an English official. Anne thought they should elope. Before they could do anything, her father sent a family friend to bring her back to England. Although Hughes was heartbroken, the breakup was probably for the best. He had wondered what they would live on, because he didn't make much money—as a poet or as a waiter. He also didn't want to depend on her father's money. Had the couple married, Hughes might have had to give up his poetry and take up mining engineering, as his father had wanted.

One morning, a knock at the door woke Hughes up. It was Alain Locke. Although they had corresponded, this was their first meeting. Like DuBois, Locke was a Harvard graduate. He was also the first African American Rhodes scholar, one the highest academic honors. Hughes was far more comfortable with sailors than with college professors.

Locke started talking about his work on a Harlem issue of the prestigious *Survey Graphic* magazine. He was also putting together an anthology of African American writing in a book called *The New Negro*. He wanted Hughes to submit work for both. He particularly liked Hughes's poem "Dream Variations," which Cullen had showed him. Hughes forgot Locke's cultured voice and stylish clothes as they talked about writing. He mentioned his interest in attending Howard University in Washington, D.C., where Locke taught. Perhaps Locke could put in a good word for him? The two men said their good-byes with plans to meet in Italy.

When the club where Hughes worked closed its doors for remodeling, it seemed like a good time to travel. Hughes left for Italy with one of his coworkers. He briefly stayed with his coworker's family in a small village, where everyone treated him as a celebrity. His friend explained that none of them had ever seen an African American before.

Hughes explored Italy for a few days before joining Locke in Venice. There, Locke appointed himself Hughes's tour guide. They rode in a gondola through the famous Grand Canal while Locke pointed out architectural highlights. Hughes was a little tired of playing tourist by the time they boarded the train to return to France. Locke sat in first class, while Langston traveled in third class. Hughes fell asleep with his money and passport pinned in his inside coat pocket. As a young boy, his grandmother had pinned his ticket and money inside his jacket so that he wouldn't lose them on the train trips to visit his mother. He had continued the practice as an adult. This time it didn't work. When he woke up in Genoa, both his money and passport were gone.

Locke returned to the United States, leaving Hughes to appeal to the American consulate in Italy for help. They recommended that he find a boat and work his way home. According to Hughes's biography, while waiting for a ship to hire him, he lived on the Genoa beach with other jobless men from other countries. Living day to day was an interesting way to get by. While waiting, he wrote what would become one of his most popular early poems, "I, Too." The poem is also known by its opening and closing line, "I, too, sing America."

Finally a ship from Philadelphia with an African American crew arrived. The captain of the *West Cawthon* hired Hughes to chip old paint off and put new paint on as they returned to America. On the way, they stopped along the coast of Spain, offering Hughes another country to explore. The *West Cawthon* arrived in New York about a month later. Hughes considered the trip a success. He wrote: ". . . ten months before, I had got to Paris with seven dollars. I had been in France, Italy, and Spain. And after the Grand Tour of the Mediterranean, I came home with a quarter, so my first European trip cost me exactly six dollars and seventy-five cents!"[6]

He must have been surprised to return home and find out that he was a famous poet. Everyone in Harlem knew about Langston Hughes, the bright young poet whose work appeared in the magazines they read. On the November evening of his return, he attended a benefit held by the NAACP. He was the star of the evening as old friends and new stopped to shake his hand. One of the many people he met that night was Carl Van Vechten. A white man twice

Langston's age, Van Vechten was well known in New York City as a flamboyant dance and music critic. He was also a photographer with a strong interest in African American culture. He later wrote articles for *Vanity Fair* magazine about spirituals and the blues. The two men couldn't have been any more different. Writer Emily Bernard, who gathered the Hughes–Van Vechten letters for *Remember Me to Harlem,* wrote: "Photographs from around 1924 reveal a large, imposing Van Vechten, with thin graying hair and generous lips that barely reached over a famously protruding pair of front teeth. His odd looks were complemented by a one-of-a-kind wardrobe that included jade bracelets, ruffled blouses, and silk lounging robes. By contrast, Langston Hughes was the definition of handsome in 1924, slender and elegant, with the dreamy looks befitting a poet."[7]

Some people were suspicious of why a white man like Van Vechten was so interested in African American culture. Although on the surface, Hughes had nothing in common with the prosperous man from the Midwest, he and Van Vechten became friends. For almost forty years, the two exchanged approximately 1,500 letters. Van Vechten always signed himself as Carlo in his letters to Hughes.

After the *Opportunity* banquet, Van Vechten took on Hughes's collected poems as a personal project. He showed the poetry to Blanche Knopf of Knopf Publishing House. Eighteen days after the *Opportunity* banquet, Knopf offered Hughes a contract for his first book of poetry, *The Weary Blues.* About Hughes's poems, Van Vechten said, "I find they have a subtle haunting quality which lingers in the memory and extraordinary sensitivity to all that is kind and lovely."[8] Van Vechten wrote the introduction to the collection. He began: "At the moment I cannot recall the name of any other person whatever who, at the age of twenty-three, has enjoyed as picturesque and rambling an existence as Langston Hughes."[9]

A few days after the NAACP banquet, Hughes would meet another important person in his life, Arna Bontemps. The newly arrived poet from California had recently had his first poetry published in the *Crisis.* The two men looked similar, which had caused some mistaken identity. Cullen's father had told his son that Hughes had arrived for a visit, when it had actually been Bontemps. The two would laugh many times about how people confused them in a friendship that was to last over forty years.

Jim Crow and Lynching

Jim Crow and lynching were heavily used practices against African Americans in the first half of the twentieth century. The phrase *Jim Crow* originally came from an 1830s song, but by the late nineteenth century it grew to mean laws and practices to keep African Americans separate from white Americans in public places. Although Jim Crow laws began in the North, they became accepted practices in the South. In many states, public places like restaurants, theaters, restrooms, and water fountains were separated according to race. For example, there would be one water fountain for white people and one for African Americans. If African Americans were allowed in a restaurant, they usually had to enter through a back door. Jim Crow was even practiced in the African American community of Harlem in the 1920s. One of its most famous clubs was the Cotton Club, which featured African American entertainers—yet African Americans weren't allowed as customers.

The Cotton Club

Jim Crow laws were a method of segregation. Segregation was made legal for a time because of a court case called *Plessy vs. Ferguson*. On June 7, 1892, a thirty-year-old shoemaker named Homer Plessy was jailed for sitting in a "white" railroad car in Louisiana. Louisiana law considered Plessy, who was one-eighth black, to be African American; therefore he was required to sit in the "colored" car. Plessy went to court and argued that the incident violated the Thirteenth and Fourteenth Amendments to the Constitution. Louisiana courts declared that the railroad company had the right to use separate cars. When the U.S. Supreme Court heard the case in 1896, it also ruled against Plessy. The court ruled that a state could require racial segregation in public facilities if the facilities offered to the two races were equal. This became known as the "separate but equal" doctrine, which led to increased segregation. "Separate but equal" kept African American children from going to white schools. The practice was abolished in 1954 with the case *Brown vs. The Board of Education of Topeka*, which declared public school segregation illegal.

The Civil Rights Act that passed in 1964 made all Jim Crow laws illegal. Ensuring that there is no segregation or discrimination is an ongoing process. When white people moved into the suburbs in the 1960s and 1970s, school district lines were often drawn to encourage segregation. The Supreme Court ordered desegregation in schools in 1973, which required busing white children to previously all-black schools and black children to white schools. Some children had to travel an hour away from home to get to school. Children in the same family would often attend separate schools. In many cases, busing proved to be impractical.

Lynching is an act of violence against a person by a mob of people who serve as prosecutor, judge, jury, and executioner. Today, we might call these people vigilantes. The term *lynching* came from a Virginia planter named Colonel Charles Lynch. In the 1700s, Lynch and his neighbors took the law into their own hands and punished British sympathizers. *Lynching* came to mean physical punishment, such as whipping or tarring and feathering. On the western frontier where there often wasn't a law officer to deal with crime, mobs lynched people for robbery or murder. Hanging became the preferred method of lynching. Before 1890, white people were more likely to be lynched. Since that time, almost all victims have been African American, although Native Americans, Latinos, Jews, and immigrants from other countries have also been lynched.

In the late nineteenth century, some people formed anti-lynching campaigns. The most effective groups were the National Association of Colored Women (NACW), the National Association for the Advancement of Colored People (NAACP), the Council for Interracial Cooperation (CIC), and the Association of Southern Women for the Prevention of Lynching (ASWPL). These people fought to stop lynching through education. They also pushed for laws against lynching. When an increasing number of white women joined the anti-lynching movement in the 1920s and 1930s, the numbers of lynchings went down. More than 3,400 known lynchings occurred against African Americans between 1882 to 1968. No lynchings have been reported since 1968.

Like many people, Hughes was horrified by lynching. He used the only weapon he had to fight it—words. "Three Songs About Lynching," published in *Opportunity*, takes three different verses that by themselves are insignificant. When the verses are joined together, the reader sees the progression from one "stage" of the lynching process to the next.

Zora Neale Hurston (left), Langston Hughes, and Jessie Fauset stand in front of a statue of Booker T. Washington in Tuskegee in 1927. Fauset was the first person to publish Hughes's work. During the Harlem Renaissance, Hurston was an up-and-coming writer with whom Hughes collaborated.

Chapter 6

Poet and Student

Langston Hughes was almost twenty-three years old when he arrived home from Europe. He had seen many things and grown up quite a bit in the three years since he'd left Columbia University. He often thought about returning to college, but felt that he could only benefit with the right school. Along with his mother and stepbrother, he was invited to Washington, D.C., to stay with cousins. The cousins were the children and grandchildren of John Mercer Langston, his grandfather's younger brother, and one of the heroes his grandmother had told him about. A lawyer and a congressman, John Mercer Langston achieved many distinctions. When he died in 1897, he left his family well provided for.

His cousins lived in the Le Droit Park area, an exclusive neighborhood for well-to-do African American doctors, lawyers, a judge, and a Methodist bishop. While everyone seemed quite impressed with his published poems in *The Crisis*, Hughes felt that they looked down on him for his shabby clothing. He had nothing but worn, faded shirts and pants, plus a sailor's pea jacket. According to Arnold Rampersad, Hughes was annoyed with his cousins' snobbish ways. "Introduced to the world of the black bourgeoisie—nowhere more exclusive than Washington—Langston found it, on the whole, insufferable."[1]

Since Hughes was interested in attending nearby Howard University, he accepted the offer to live with them. Surely his great-uncle's affiliation with the university as the first law school dean, plus his acquaintance with Professor Alain Locke, would help him get a scholarship. Hughes was disappointed when he was turned down. If he wanted to go to college, he would have to save his money.

Hughes took a job with a weekly African American newspaper, but when he found out that his job was not to write but to sell advertising, he quit. He looked into other jobs recommended by his cousins, but lacked the qualifications to work at such places as the prestigious Library of Congress. Broke, Langston took a job at a laundry sorting dirty clothes. It paid $12 a week, the most he had ever earned. His relatives were embarrassed that he worked there. Their continued arrogance upset Carrie so much that one day they moved out of the fashionable home and into a couple of furnished rooms in a brick house on S Street near the laundry. They shared an oil stove that winter, carrying it back and forth between their rooms for heat. Prices were high in Washington, D.C., and Hughes couldn't save any money. Once again, his unhappiness drove him to write poetry. He described this period in his life in *The Big Sea*. "My two years in Washington were unhappy years, except for poetry and the friends I made through poetry. I wrote many poems. I always put them away new for several weeks in a bottom drawer. Then I would take them out and re-read them. If they seemed bad, I would throw them away. They would all seem good when I wrote them and, usually, bad when I would look at them again. So most of them were thrown away."[2]

Hughes liked to walk along Seventh Street, a ghetto for poor African Americans. This was the only neighborhood in Washington, D.C., where African Americans could go to restaurants or the theater in the very segregated city. On Seventh Street, Hughes met what he called the "low down folks." He heard music on the street—blues, jazz, and gospel at the storefront churches—and he continued creating blues poems like he had in Paris. He often sang them on the way to work until one day a man asked him if he was ill because it sounded like he was groaning!

He had long been drawn to the blues, a type of music he described as sadder than gospel. Hughes helped Carl Van Vechten with a series of articles on the blues for *Vanity Fair* magazine. He tried to explain what the blues meant to him in a letter to Van Vechten: "Perhaps the reason the Blues seems so melancholy to me is that I first heard them sung as a child by a blind orchestra that used to wander about the streets of the slums and the red-light district in Kansas City, singing for nickels or pennies, a fish sandwich, or anything one chose to give."[3]

Hughes lost the job at the laundry when he missed a week of work because of illness. A friend of his mother's put in a good word for him with Dr. Carter G. Woodson. A child of slaves, Dr. Woodson distinguished himself by earning a PhD from Harvard. He was an author and editor of the *Journal of Negro History*, and he had founded the Association for the Study of Negro Life and History.

Woodson's current project was compiling a list of 30,000 people for an account of "Free Negro Heads of Families in the United States in 1830." Woodson hired Hughes as his personal assistant.

Although Hughes admired what Dr. Woodson was trying to do, he didn't like the job. He didn't like being cooped up in a small room and proofing the information until his eyes hurt. His position didn't leave much time for writing. He didn't stay long. His next job was as a busboy at the Wardman Park Hotel in Washington, D.C. One day, Hughes heard that a famous poet he had studied in high school, Vachel Lindsay, would be giving a reading at the hotel. People called Lindsay the troubadour poet because of his theatrical performance of his works. Hughes had been trying to get more notice for his poetry and wondered if Lindsay could help. When Hughes spotted Lindsay in the hotel dining room, he told the famous poet of his admiration and quickly dropped some of his own poems next to Lindsay's plate.

When Vachel Lindsay gave his reading that night, he told the audience about the African American poet working as a busboy. Then he read aloud the three poems that Hughes had left by his plate: "Jazzonia," "Negro Dancers," and "The Weary Blues." The following day, newspapers came to take pictures and interview the African American busboy who wrote poetry admired by Vachel Lindsay. When Lindsay checked out of the hotel, he left Hughes a kind note and a copy of Amy Lowell's biography of John Keats.

Things began looking up for Hughes. After his articles for *Vanity Fair,* Van Vechten encouraged the magazine to publish Hughes's poetry. Hughes won another poetry contest offered by *The Crisis.* Joel Spingarn had established the Spingarn Medal in 1914 to award African American achievement. Hughes also met Joel's brother, Arthur. Arthur Spingarn would become Hughes's friend and attorney for the remainder of his life.

After his poetry contest win, Mrs. Spingarn invited Langston to her elegant home for tea. He told her about his dream of returning to college. She said she would see what she could do to help him. On Christmas Eve in 1925, Hughes received a letter from Amy Spingarn telling him to make plans for college; she had set aside $300 to help him.

Disillusioned with Howard University and Washington, D.C., Hughes had heard from a poet acquaintance of another college that sounded perfect. Lincoln University was a small school of about 300 students located in rolling farmland forty-five miles southwest of Philadelphia. Hughes called it the "backwoods" of Pennsylvania. This all-male (it would become open to women in 1952) African

57

American university, founded by white abolitionists in 1854, graduated more doctors, ministers, and lawyers than any other African American college. With many professors having ties to Princeton University, Lincoln was sometimes referred to as the "black Princeton."

Friends Jessie Fauset and Countee Cullen objected to his attending the old, rundown university in the Pennsylvania countryside, but Hughes loved it and started in February. The only way to get there was to travel on a milk train route, where the train stopped at every house to deliver milk. Once the train arrived at the Lincoln station, there was still a mile to walk to reach the school. Hughes explained to Van Vechten, "You see, I'm going into seclusion, weary of the world. . . . And I hope nobody there reads poetry. My own poems are about to bore me to death, I've heard them so much in the mouths of others recently."[4]

A few weeks before Hughes started school, *The Weary Blues* collection was released to excellent reviews. *The New York Times* called Hughes a "natural troubadour" and wrote: "We sincerely hope that Langston Hughes will receive the wide reading he deserves. . . . If he can go on as he has begun, America bids fair to have a poet worthy of far more than passing mention."[5]

Countee Cullen had less praise for Hughes's book. In a review in *Opportunity* magazine, Cullen said that Hughes put too much emphasis on African American themes. Others obviously didn't agree, as the book went into a second printing after only four months. Still, his friend's negative review angered Hughes, who responded in *The Nation* with an essay titled "The Negro Artist and the Racial Mountain." He said he felt pity for an African American poet he knew who wanted to be known as a "poet," not as a "Negro poet." In his eyes, surrendering racial pride was the same as wanting to be white. He wrote, "The road for the serous black artist, then, who would produce a racial art is most certainly rocky and the mountain is high."[6]

Lincoln was small enough that most everyone knew each other. Daily life was casual. No one dressed up except on Sundays. Hughes enjoyed what he referred to as "plain and solid" food. The students enjoyed playing tricks on one another. As sophomores, they would shave the heads of the freshman students.

Hughes played the writer on weekends. He often read his poems in New York City, but sometimes traveled other places as well. One highlight was reading at his old high school in Cleveland. His old friend, Sartur, came to hear him.

That summer, Hughes moved to Harlem and began to write short stories. *The Messenger* published his first short stories for $10 each. With a group of writers that included Wallace Thurman, editor of the *Messenger*; Zora Neale Hurston; and

Gwendolyn Bennett, Hughes decided to publish a quarterly magazine focusing on young African American writers and artists. It was to be called *Fire!!,* after one of Hughes's poems. Financial problems shut the magazine down after one issue.

Meanwhile, Hughes explored other types of writing and found he enjoyed writing lyrics. He wrote lyrics for musical theater (*O Blues!*), and lyrics for two of blues composer W. C. Handy's songs. He also spent time learning about people with both African American and white blood. Biographer Faith Berry writes, "This, the tragic mulatto theme, which had appeared earlier in the poem 'Cross,' was to engage him time and again for several years, and his second poetic treatment of it came that summer of 1926. The poem was 'Mulatto.'"[7]

During his second year at Lincoln, his second book of poetry, *Fine Clothes to the Jew,* was published. He later grew to regret the title, although he explained it to Jewish friends like the Spingarns and in his autobiography. "I called it *Fine Clothes to the Jew,* because the first poem, 'Hard Luck,' a blues, was about a man who was often so broke he had no recourse but to pawn his clothes—to take them, as the Negroes say, to the 'the Jew's' or to 'Uncle's.'"[8]

Alain Locke introduced him to Charlotte Mason at a Carnegie Hall concert soon after Hughes's twenty-fifth birthday. Mrs. Mason was a very wealthy seventy-three-year-old who had met Locke at a lecture he'd given on African art. Hughes visited the white-haired woman at her Park Avenue home at her request over Easter weekend. They got along well. When he said his good-byes, she pressed a fifty-dollar bill into his hand. A month later in 1927, Charlotte Mason became Langston's patron. It was not unusual in this time period for writers and artists to have a patron who would financially support and advise the writer or artist. Patrons tended to be white and quite rich. Mrs. Mason directed Hughes and others she supported to call her "Godmother."

Each month, Mrs. Mason sent Hughes $150 plus extra things like food and paper for his writing. In return, he was to consult with her about what he was writing. He was also required to send her an itemized account of his expenses, something that certainly must have reminded him of his father. And just as before, his accounting was made more difficult when his mother regularly asked for money.

At first, Mrs. Mason seemed like a surrogate mother, giving him all the things his own mother never could. Hughes mentioned being worried about his stepbrother, Kit, who was two years behind in school and getting more rebellious every day. Hughes blamed his mother, who spoiled him. Mrs. Mason found Kit a good foster home and school. (Carrie removed him from the foster home soon afterward).

After a while, Mrs. Mason's demands grew. She expected Hughes to escort her to social events when he was in New York. She tried to choose the books he read, the music he listened to, and the plays he saw. She also demanded to see everything he wrote. One thing he didn't show her, but published nine years later, was "Poet to Patron." The poem ended:

> A factory shift's better,
> A week's meager pay,
> Than a perfumed note asking
> What poems today?[9]

Van Vechten had been encouraging Hughes to work on his autobiography, but what he really wanted to do was work on a novel. He began the story of an African American boy growing up in the Midwest; largely it was his own story he was writing. Mrs. Mason even hired a stenographer, Louise Thompson, to help him. The novel, *Not Without Laughter,* was published in 1930, a year after he graduated from Lincoln University.

Hughes took a brief vacation to Cuba. Upon returning, he began collaborating with another of Mrs. Mason's protégés, Zora Neale Hurston. They had first met the night of the *Opportunity* banquet. He enjoyed being with Hurston, a skilled storyteller who collected African American folktales.

The two writers began working on a play based on a story called "The Bone of Contention." They titled their play *Mule Bone,* but decided to keep their collaboration a secret from everyone but Mrs. Mason and Louise Thompson, who was typing for them. Thompson became another good friend to Hughes. They had similar upbringings, and both took great pride in being African American. After a break in writing, Hughes tried to contact Hurston about finishing the play, but she didn't return his phone calls.

In May, Hughes planned a trip to Washington, D.C. Mrs. Mason said he should stay home and write. When Hughes insisted on going, she became furious and refused to support him any longer. He was apologetic, but she refused to talk to him other than to say that he would most certainly fail as a writer without her help. As he had on his first visit to his father, Hughes became severely ill. It was as if he were holding in so much anger, it made him sick.

He visited his mother, who was living once again in Cleveland, and decided to look up his old friends, the Jelliffes. They still ran the theater, the Karamu House. The Jelliffes told him that they had come across a play they were thinking of producing, written by Zora Neale Hurston. Did Hughes know her? Shocked, he took a look at the play and discovered it was *Mule Bone*. Hurston was passing off their play as solely her own work. When Hurston refused to talked to him, he tried to enlist Van Vechten's help, writing, "The Gilpin Players, probably the best Little Theater Negro group in the country, must open downtown with this play on February 15th, [1931, approximately a month away], so you see how pushed for time they are. The play came to them through [Samuel] French quite without my knowledge, and bearing only Zora's name, but in such a confused form that I don't see how the Guild or anybody else read it."[10]

Van Vechten insisted on staying out of the matter. According to Hughes, Hurston went from refusing to talk to him to angrily accusing him of trying to cheat her. Author Faith Berry suggests that Hurston might have been jealous of Louise Thompson, as she reportedly accused Hughes of including her as a coauthor. Hughes had said nothing of the kind, but decided to ask for help from his friend and lawyer, Arthur Spingarn.

There are many sides to this story. Hughes's biographers indicate that the matter was somehow tied into the situation with Mrs. Mason, who still served as Hurston's patron as well as Alain Locke's.

When Mrs. Mason terminated her patronage with Hughes in 1930, both Hurston and Locke supported the decision. They told her about his rather large ego and how he hadn't appreciated her. Apparently, Mrs. Mason was anti-Semitic, so she also didn't like hearing about Hughes's Jewish lawyer either. Saddened by what his old friends were doing, Hughes became permanently estranged from both of them.

Hughes tried one more time to tell his side of the story to Mrs. Mason. When she refused to listen, he washed his hands of the whole affair. "As soon as I got rid of the last dollar of the money left from my estranged patron's allowances, I felt immensely better. My stomach, that for weeks had turned over and over since my relations with the kind and elderly lady on Park Avenue had ended so abruptly, now stopped turning over altogether."[11]

After three years, their patron-writer relationship had ended. Hughes would never seek out a patron again. He decided that the only person he wanted to answer to from then on was himself.

The Blues

The blues, which gets its name from lyrics that focus on sadness or loneliness, is one of the first truly American forms of music. African Americans created the blues when they combined African sounds with European music. Traditional blues lyrics consist of several three-line verses. The second line of each verse repeats the first line, sometimes with slight changes. The third line responds to the first two lines in rhyme. Writer Bill Dahl describes the blues as being more than rules for notes and verses, however. He says that the blues is all about feeling. The blues might be about feeling down, but they could also make people laugh about their "blues." Langston Hughes wrote, "The blues are folk-songs born of heartache."[12]

The blues are simple, yet complex. Verses and musical notes may be repeated over and over, yet the blues is also about technique, lyrics, and emotion. It is believed that the blues may have developed after the Civil War. Plantation workers in the South once used short calls and wails to communicate with one another. These calls and wails were called "field hollers." Ring shouts are the combined singing and movement in spirituals. Singing, hand clapping, foot stamping, and thigh slapping were all part of ring shouts. Blues probably developed from field hollers and the ring shouts of spirituals.

By the late 1800s, country blues could be heard in the Mississippi Delta region. A male singer sang the blues, usually accompanied by an acoustic guitar, played with complicated fingerpicking. Although the focus was on the vocals, instruments began to take on greater importance. Acoustic guitars were traded for electric guitars. Performers developed new techniques like the "bottleneck slide," where a guitarist would scrape a knife or glass bottleneck up the guitar neck to sound like moaning. Today, hollow brass slides worn on the finger accomplish the same effect.

As African Americans migrated in large numbers to the North in the early twentieth century, they brought the blues with them. The blues became a popular music form in diverse communities in the early 1900s, thanks in part to the efforts of bandleader W. C. Handy, who wrote songs like "Memphis Blues." Hughes called Handy's "St. Louis Blues" the best

Bessie Smith

blues song ever written. Vaudeville singer Mamie Smith recorded the first blues record, "Crazy Blues," in February 1920, and white audiences began to listen. Bessie Smith, known as the empress of the blues, exposed this new music to an even wider audience. Other early contributors were artists such as Billie Holiday and Charlie Parker.

The blues began to show geographical distinctions. Early blues came from the delta region of Mississippi, commonly known as the birthplace of the blues. Delta blues became known by the passionate slide guitar and vocals, producing blues legends Muddy Waters and Elmore James. Texas blues, first heard in the 1920s, used acoustic guitar as an extra vocal. After World War II, Texas blues adopted the electric guitar and began using horns. Chicago blues added drums, bass, piano, and sometimes saxophones in the later 1940s. This style still focused on the lead guitar because of performers like B.B. King. East Coast blues might use complex fingerpicking or a jazz sound with more horns. In the 1950s, harmonica blues developed, as the harmonica was played into a microphone. Modern electric blues takes the blues of the past and gives it a more complex chord and a rock or funk beat.

The blues is flexible and always evolving. Unique styles like urban blues, boogie woogie, and rhythm and blues have emerged. The blues has also influenced every other type of music—classical, jazz, country music, and especially rock and roll and hip-hop. Many of today's performers, such as noted guitarist Eric Clapton, recognize the influence of the blues on their work.

Men make their way to Haiti's Citadelle Laferrière in 1939, just a few years after Hughes and Ingram toured the site. The fortress was built between 1805 and 1820 by Haitian leader Henri Christophe to protect the newly independent nation from French attacks. It could house thousands of soldiers and was protected by 365 cannons. The massive monument remains the national symbol of Haiti.

Chapter
7

Speaking to the South

The United States was in the midst of the Great Depression in 1930. Opportunities were few, but Hughes needed to get far away from Mrs. Mason and Zora Neale Hurston. When he won the William E. Harmon Award for Distinguished Achievement in literature among African Americans for his first novel, *Not Without Laughter,* he found the means to do so. The award included a gold medal and $400. It was the largest award he had ever won. After giving $100 to his mother, Hughes decided the best use for the remaining money was to visit the Caribbean, sit on the beach, and think about what direction he wanted his life to take. "I needed sun,"[1] he said in *The Big Sea.* He had met an artist, Zell Ingram, through the Jelliffes. Like Hughes, Ingram was an old Central High graduate. They headed for Florida in Zell's mother's Ford. From there, they planned to visit Cuba and Haiti.

Hughes and Ingram stopped in Daytona Beach to visit educator Mary McLeod Bethune, a lifelong fighter against racism and adviser on education. When she talked, Presidents listened. Hughes had met Mrs. Bethune when she gave a talk at Columbia while he was a student there. She had founded a college for African Americans, Bethune-Cookman College, in Daytona Beach, Florida. Bethune kindly listened to Langston's worries and offered him food and a guest room. The next day he read some of his poems to one of her English classes.

After arriving in southern Florida, Hughes and Ingram took the first boat available to African Americans for Havana, Cuba. This was Langston's third trip to the city. The first time he had been while working on a ship. He had also

65

visited the previous year, looking for a composer to help him with an opera. By the time of this visit, Hughes saw Havana as a place where he had many friends. One of these was Nicholás Guillén, Cuba's future national poet. Even the newspaper welcomed Hughes to Cuba with a headline that translated to "The Poet Langston Hughes Visits Us Again." Much of his work had been translated into Spanish, and he enjoyed his reputation as a great writer in Cuba.

Most of this trip was enjoyable; unfortunately, racism had followed them from the United States. In one incident, the two men were refused admission into a dance hall. Near the end of their visit, they were refused entrance to a section of beach controlled by white Americans. The white Americans called the police, who arrested Hughes and Ingram for trespassing. A police officer told them that problems like this had started when white Americans had come to Cuba. The judge dismissed the case.

After being released, they left for Haiti. Hughes recalled stories his grandmother once told him about Haiti, the world's first black republic—how the dark-skinned natives didn't want to be slaves any longer and overthrew the light-skinned French people. The symbol of the Haitians' desire for independence became the Citadel, a fortress they built to keep the French from renewing attacks. Stretching across a mountain peak with sheer cliffs on three sides, the only accessible side was protected by hundreds of cannons. Seeing the Citadel had long been a goal of Langston's. He was properly impressed with the majestic symbol of freedom.

The image of the Citadel contrasted with what Hughes saw in the city of Port-au-Prince during the 1931 summer. The degree of poverty was one he never knew existed. Children lined the streets—diseased, starving, and without shoes. Hughes discovered a strong division among classes that related to shoes. Light-skinned middle and upper classes in Haiti wore shoes; the darker lower classes did not. "Most of Haiti's people without shoes could not read or write, and had no power. They lived in thatched huts or rickety homes; rose with the sun; went to sleep with the dark. They washed their clothes in running streams with lathery weeds—too poor to buy soap."[2] Hughes would write an essay, "People Without Shoes," that *New Masses* published the following October.

Returning home through Cuba, Hughes realized he was being followed by a strange man. When he told this to a Cuban journalist friend, the friend suggested that the government might think Hughes was a communist. The government at that time was suspicious of communists. It wouldn't be the last time Hughes was followed with suspicions that he was a communist. In the United States, the

Federal Bureau of Investigation (FBI) would be keeping a close eye on him during the 1940s and 1950s.

Back in America, the Depression dragged on. The Depression was hard on most people, but no group was hit harder than African Americans. By 1932, approximately half of the African American population was out of work. According to Rampersad, "Hughes concentrated now on expressing his radical opinion about the economic crisis gripping the country. A recent Urban League study showed national black unemployment at disastrous levels."[3]

Hughes began to be more vocal about discrimination. Because of his increasing interest in politics and the fact that many of his works were published in socialist magazines like *New Masses,* he developed a reputation as a communist. He appreciated some points of socialism and saw the possibility of true equality for African Americans under that form of government, but he denied being a communist. He believed that that alliance would conflict with his being a writer.

Hughes now had a goal. He didn't want to work on ships or in laundries or as a busboy. He had two books of poetry and a novel published. His poems had appeared in more than twenty anthologies and had been translated into several foreign languages. He decided the next step was to make a living solely from his writing, something no African American writer had ever done. He found his inspiration from Mary McLeod Bethune. Perhaps the kind woman represented the mother he wished he had. Bethune praised Langston's writing and encouraged him to write more. Inspired by her success, Langston wrote a poem praising African American motherhood, which touched her very much. He called it *The Negro Mother.* The following lines may have been written for her:

> *Three hundred years in the deepest South:*
> *But God put a song and a prayer in my mouth.*
> *God put a dream like steel in my soul.*
> *Now, through my children, I'm reaching the goal.* [4]

Bethune told Hughes, "Why don't you tour the South reading your poems? Thousands of Negro students would be proud and inspired by seeing you and hearing you. You are young, but you have already made a name for yourself in literary circles, and you can help black students to feel that a Negro youth can amount to something in this world in spite of our problems."[5]

Hughes's Harlem friends were aghast. Travel in the South? Where discrimination was rampant and often dangerous to African Americans? Yet Hughes

67

wanted to share his work with the large African American population of the South and bring young people the message that they could succeed also. Needing help to finance his poetry readings there, he applied to the Julius Rosenwald Foundation, started by a president of Sears, Roebuck, and Company with the purpose of making a more equal society. Hughes also wrote the presidents of African American colleges in the South. Almost immediately, they wrote back to say they would love to have him speak to their students.

Penniless, he stayed with his Aunt Toy and her musician husband at their St. Nicholas Avenue apartment while waiting for word about the Rosenwald. Toy Harper had grown up with Hughes's mother in Kansas, running off as a teen to be in show business. Her singing and dancing were nothing special, so she ended up designing clothes for theatrical productions. Toy had always treated Hughes like a member of her family and always supported him. She was even at his first book signing for *The Weary Blues*, and he would dedicate *The Big Sea* to the Harpers. They were some of the few people he trusted in his life.

While making preparations, his mind dwelled on the latest controversy from the South. As he and Ingram had headed to Florida to start their Caribbean trip, they heard about a white mob in Alabama dragging nine young African American men to the Scottsboro jail. The young men were accused and convicted of rape, though the truth of the charges was doubtful. Hughes began writing about the incident. First, there was a poem titled "Scottsboro" that was published in *Opportunity* magazine. He also wrote an interactive play that used audience participation. It was called *Scottsboro, Limited: A One Act Play*. It was a powerful piece featuring a single chair sitting on a platform on a bare stage. The attention of the audience was directed to the chair . . . the electric chair. At the end of the play, the chair is smashed. Hughes combined four of his poems with *Scottsboro Limited* to raise money for the boys' defense. Another effort to raise money took place in San Francisco when he organized an auction emceed by actor James Cagney. Those proceeds also went to the defense fund.

Hughes's chief concern about his trip to the South was travel, a significant problem for African Americans. Arna Bontemps once wrote to Hughes, "This is one of those days on which I want to swear to leave the South behind, forever. While I see improvements almost every day in some quarters, I can't help getting mad when travel is involved. . . . I'm having trouble getting train reservations to my Greensboro engagement. Will try to get a plane. If none is available, will be tempted to cancel—though I do hate to put the folks on a spot. What I hate most about such an experience is the feeling of depression it induces."[6]

The grant from the Rosenwald Foundation came through. Hughes purchased a new Model A Ford to get from place to place, even though he couldn't drive it. He hired a college friend from Lincoln to be his driver and manager. With a small booklet of poems titled *The Negro Mother* and copies of *The Weary Blues,* they left in October.

Hughes's tour started in Philadelphia. His first official stop of the South was at Virginia State College, where his great-uncle John Mercer Langston had served as the first president. The tour would also take him to Florida, Georgia, Louisiana, Alabama, Texas, and North Carolina. *The Negro Mother* received positive feedback wherever he went. In Alabama, he was invited to Booker T. Washington's Tuskegee Institute, where he met inventor George Washington Carver and toured his lab.

Hughes met many gracious people on his tour of the South, but when he wanted to talk about the Scottsboro situation, the Southern people refused to talk out of fear for their own safety. Hughes met with the young men at Kilby Prison on the outskirts of Montgomery, Alabama. The second floor held the cells for those on death row. Not one of those prisoners was white. Hughes read some of his poems to the young men, but felt that poetry at such a time was futile.

He needed to express his feelings about the situation. He believed these young men, boys really, were not guilty. Frustrated, he wrote a poem called "Christ in Alabama." The poem attacked organized religion for its failure to help poor people of color. "It was an ironic poem inspired by the thought of how Christ, with no human father, would be accepted were He born in the South of a Negro mother,"[7] he wrote in his second autobiography, *I Wonder as I Wander.*

The poem upset people of both races in the South. Hughes had only one scheduled appearance at a white school, the University of North Carolina at Chapel Hill. He was greeted by an angry mob, who believed that "Christ in Alabama" was blasphemous. With guards nearby, he spoke to a packed house of people. Even though the tension in the room was strong, the audience applauded "The Negro Mother," and the booklet sold out. However, the university refused to pay him for his appearance. They said it was because of the publication of "Christ in Alabama" in *Contempo,* an unofficial magazine published by Chapel Hill students.

Scottsboro

Scottsboro was a small town in Alabama. Since the 1930s, *Scottsboro* also has referred to several civil rights cases that grew out of events near this town. No other case has produced so many trials, convictions, and retrials as did the Scottsboro civil rights trials.

On March 25, 1931, the South Railroad freight train was running from Chattanooga to Memphis. During the Depression, hitching rides was a popular pastime for vagrants and teens alike. It was also a means to travel cheaply to look for work. About two dozen white and African American teens were on the train that day. Four of the African American teens were checking on possible government jobs in Memphis. Four white teens, two girls and two boys, had also been job hunting at Chattanooga's cotton mills. Soon after the train crossed the Alabama border, a white boy walked across the top of a tank car, stepping on the hand of a black teen named Haywood Patterson. Two groups of boys, one white and one African American, began throwing rocks at each other. After the white teens were forced off the train, some went to the stationmaster to report being attacked by the African American boys. Further down the track, the train stopped at

Paint Rock, Alabama, where a group of armed men rushed at the train and grabbed every African American they could find. They tied nine teenagers together with plow line, loaded them on to a flatbed truck, and took them to the Scottsboro jail.

Two white girls told the men that they had been raped by a gang of armed African American teens. One of the girls pointed out six of the nine boys. One of the boys, Clarence Norris, was struck by a bayonet when he called the

Clarence Norris

70

girl a liar. A guard decided that the other boys must have raped the other girl. Several hundred men gathered that night, intent on lynching the boys, but Alabama's governor had ordered the National Guard to Scottsboro to protect the suspects.

Trials for the teens began twelve days after their arrest in the courtroom of Judge A. E. Hawkins. Two unprepared and unqualified lawyers represented the boys. They cross-examined one of the girls for only a couple of minutes and didn't question the examining physicians at all. Although there were contradictions between the girls' testimonies, they weren't questioned further. The only witnesses for the defense were the boys, whom no one believed. The Alabama courts quickly convicted the nine teens, sentencing them to die. One was only twelve years old.

The Supreme Court overturned the convictions, saying that the teens had not received adequate representation by lawyers. In 1933, Alabama began a case against Haywood Patterson. Interested in the case, the Communist party hired a prominent non-communist lawyer, Samuel Leibowitz, to represent him. Although one of the girls admitted she had not been raped, a jury still convicted Patterson of the crime. The judge, unhappy with the verdict, ordered a third trial. In it, Patterson and another teen, Clarence Norris, were again convicted. The Supreme Court overturned these convictions because the law reads that a person should be tried by a jury of their peers, and African Americans were not allowed to serve on Alabama juries.

The trials gained worldwide attention, with many believing that the young men had been accused only because they were African American. Alabama officials dropped the charges in four cases but insisted on trying the others. The five remaining young men were found guilty and sent to prison. By 1950, four of the five had been paroled; the fifth escaped to Michigan where the governor refused to release him to Alabama authorities. The Scottsboro cases focused worldwide attention on discrimination against African Americans in the South.

Hughes (right) sits with his lifelong friend, Arna Bontemps. After meeting in the 1920s, the men became frequent collaborators and corresponded for over forty years.

Chapter 8

War and Death

One high point of Hughes's trip through the South was seeing Arna Bontemps. Unable to support his wife and children on a writer's pay, Bontemps had taken a job teaching at Oakwood Junior College in Huntsville, Alabama. Since their first meeting seven years earlier, the two writers had seen little of each other. Hughes spent an enjoyable Christmas with the Bontemps family. "The reunion with his look-alike, Arna Bontemps, would be another major step toward his future. Although the young men had known each other since the end of 1924, their meeting in December 1931 would mark the start of a deeper relationship, virtually a marriage of minds, that would last without the slightest friction until Hughes's death thirty-six years later,"[1] said biographer Arnold Rampersad.

Hughes valued the normalcy of Bontemps's life. The two friends talked about working on a book together—a book for children. They outlined the story of *Popo and Fifina*, about a Haitian brother and sister. Bontemps submitted it to Macmillan Publishing, where it was immediately accepted.

After his stay with Bontemps, Hughes stopped at the University of Kansas, where he was overwhelmed by his memories of growing up in Lawrence with his grandmother. He thought about his parents as he spoke at Langston University in Oklahoma, where his parents had met thirty-four years previously.

Hughes's reading tour took him through the western United States to California. The sunny state was more accepting of the African American poet than the discriminatory Texas, New Mexico, and Arizona. While in California, he received an invitation to participate in making a movie in the Soviet Union, along with other African Americans. The movie project was to be about the American labor movement and race relations. Soviet filmmakers wanted Hughes to work on the dialogue and perhaps act in the movie. Many young white writers his age wrote for Hollywood, an opportunity he knew was closed to him because of race. "It was my intention to try very hard to make a living as a professional writer, so I was interested in all fields of writing. But I thought if I were ever to work in motion pictures or learn about them, it would have to be abroad, so I canceled the few engagements I had pending in the Middle West to sail for Europe,"[2] Hughes wrote in *I Wonder As I Wander.*

Rushing to New York, Hughes caught the S.S. *Europa* to the Soviet Union just in time. Toy Harper saw his ship off. In addition to his clothing, he had packed a typewriter and a phonograph for playing the big box of record albums that followed him everywhere: works by Bessie Smith, Duke Ellington, and Louis Armstrong. His excitement was like what he had felt when going to Africa. He recalled his Jewish classmates at Central High School talking about the new Soviet Union after the people overthrew the czarist regime in 1917. Had the Soviet Union achieved equality?

He joined more than twenty other African Americans on board, including Louise Thompson and Alain Locke. It's not clear what Locke was doing on the ship, as he wasn't part of the film project. According to Berry, Locke continued writing to Charlotte Mason about Hughes's activities. Hughes acted as if Locke's presence meant nothing to him. He had cut ties with Locke at the same time as Hurston and Mason.

In the Soviet Union, no one shut doors on or refused service to any of the African Americans. Instead, the Soviets went out of their way to be helpful. It was probably the first time any of the Americans had seen a white person give up their bus seat for an African American. Hughes wrote, "On a crowded bus, nine times out of ten, some Russian would say, *'Negrochanski tovarish'*—Negro comrade—take my seat!"[3] The thirty-year-old poet, and now screenwriter, was inspired to write radical verse. The best known is "Good Morning, Revolution," a parody of Carl Sandburg's poem "Good Morning, America."

Hughes was disappointed when he saw the script for *Black and White,* based on a poem by the leading poet of the Russian Revolution, Vladimir Mayakovsky. The film was about African American steelworkers in Birmingham, Alabama. The workers and the progressive labor organizer were the heroes. The villains were the white bosses. However, the script was so unrealistic about life for African Americans that it was laughable. Problems with the script were only one of

Hughes (left) with an unidentified man, in what was known as the Soviet Union in 1932. Believing the Soviet Union to be free of racism, Hughes spent a year in this country writing his most radical verse.

many delays. Eventually, the film was canceled. Rumors spread that the Soviets feared the reaction of the American government.

While most of his group returned to America, Hughes decided to stay in the Soviet Union. Work in America had been a gamble, but he had plenty of work in the Soviet Union, writing for socialist magazines and assisting in translations. One thing he was particularly proud of was a series contrasting African Americans with the darker races of the Soviet Union for the daily newspaper *Izvestia*. Rampersad noted, "Hughes felt the freedom of Russia at least as intensely; for the first time in his life, he could live by his writing, and handsomely so."[4]

Hughes learned to speak Russian. While exploring the central Asian republics of the Soviet Union, he met Arthur Koestler, a Jewish Hungarian writer best known for a prison novel called *Darkness at Noon*. Glad to have someone with whom to speak English, the two writers traveled together for a while. Koestler told Hughes that he saw many problems with Soviet communism. He later wrote of meeting Langston Hughes in his own autobiography, *The Invisible Writing*.

Hughes also started another romantic relationship. Sylvia Chen, a Chinese dancer, performed both traditional Chinese dances and the modern styles popularized by Isadora Duncan. When she met Hughes, she was studying choreography and specializing as an interpreter of Asian dances. The relationship didn't go anywhere, although he wrote in his second autobiography of falling in love with Chen. Perhaps he wasn't interested in a serious relationship, as he was also reportedly seeing a Soviet actress. Hughes and Chen wrote letters occasionally until Chen married another American in 1936. Hughes biographer Faith Berry interviewed Chen in 1977. Chen said that Hughes was a difficult person to know and that the only thing he was committed to was his work.

First Anne Coussey, and now Sylvia. Some speculated as to why Langston never married or at least have a long-term romantic relationship. Some said he was homosexual, but those who knew him best simply said that Hughes was married to his work. According to Rampersad, "Hughes knew he could not marry. Certain only of the solace of poetry and motion, he would not encumber himself. Which is perhaps the same as saying that he could not give himself, and thus could not finally possess any of the women who were drawn by his successes, his handsome face, and his winning ways."[5]

After a year in the Soviet Union, Hughes left on June 17, 1933, returning home by a different route. He traveled across Asia to China and Japan. To his surprise and irritation, police in Japan monitored and even interrogated him. With his reputation for leftist, even communist, ties, the Japanese police were worried about Hughes's earlier visit to the strongly communist China.

When he arrived back in California, Hughes was ready to sell nonfiction and poems about his year in the Soviet Union. No one was interested. Although Hughes would never go so far as to join the Communist party, he promoted many communist ideals and politicians. He believed communism offered the most to African Americans. Carl Van Vechten had no interest in the radical verse and essays. Neither did his usual publisher, Knopf. Blanche Knopf had already turned over the business of Hughes's manuscripts to a literary agent named Maxim Lieber. Hughes was happy with Lieber, an affirmed socialist, who aggressively placed his work.

A wealthy acquaintance in California, Noel Sullivan, offered Hughes the use of his cottage in Carmel-by-the-Sea for writing. Called Ennesfree, the two-bedroom cottage provided great views of the Pacific Ocean. Hughes had recently read D.H. Lawrence, which inspired him to write his own short stories. He told Bontemps, "The era of trials and tribulations is indeed upon the world. The only good thing about suffering is that it gives you something to write about after-wards."[6]

Hughes wrote and took walks with Sullivan's German shepherd, which came with the cottage. After about a year, he had a collection of short stories, *The Ways of White Folks,* published in 1934. His reputation continued to develop, both as a writer and as an advocate for African Americans. *The New York Daily Mirror* included him on their list of the 25 Most Interesting People, joining icons like Franklin Roosevelt and Will Rogers. Even so, Hughes never had much money. He sent every cent he could spare to his mother, who complained that it was never enough.

An anti-communist tide began sweeping in the country in the late 1930s. When people in Carmel started grumbling about labor problems, Hughes felt as if he were becoming the symbol of the political left and, as such, attracting negative attention. He left for Nevada, where he applied for a Guggenheim Fellowship so that he could continue writing. Meanwhile, he began writing anything he thought might make him some money. He wrote nonracial love stories under the pen name of David Boatman, but was unhappy doing so. One day while out walking, he came across a small cemetery and saw what looked like a mailbox. He thought "Mail Box for the Dead" would make a great title for a short story. He began writing the story. According to his autobiography, he began thinking of his father at this time, something he rarely did.

On November 5, Hughes received a letter written two weeks earlier by his father's friends, the Patiño sisters. They reported that James Hughes was seriously ill and that Hughes should come to Mexico immediately. As he was packing and borrowing money to get to Mexico, another letter from the Patiños arrived. His father had died.

Hughes arrived in Mexico with the intention of managing his father's affairs. He learned that his father had not mentioned him in his will. James Hughes had left everything to the Patiños. Apologetic, the sisters offered to share with him. Hughes shrugged off any disappointment he might have felt. He had not had a good relationship with his father, yet Hughes might have accepted a mention in the will as proof that his father had loved him. He had never heard words of love or praise from his father.

Without any other plans, he decided to stay awhile in Mexico. He attended bullfights, made friends, and translated works by Mexican authors. Six months later, in 1936, word came that he had won the Guggenheim Fellowship. Hughes returned to America with many plans. One of these was writing for the theater.

He worked on several plays with his old friends, the Jelliffes, at the Karamu House in Cleveland. His 1935 play, *Mulatto,* altered by the director, had already opened to poor reviews. His attention, however, was elsewhere as he traveled to Oberlin, Ohio. His mother had been diagnosed with breast cancer. All of his money and resources went toward Carrie's treatment. Hughes wrote other plays that were moderate successes. The Gilpin Players in Cleveland put on his comedy *Little Ham.* He also wrote a historical drama called *Emperor of Haiti.*

Through his work in the theater, he met Elsie Roxborough, a playwright twelve years his junior. They may have had a brief romantic relationship before they lost contact two years later.

Hughes was summoned across the ocean once more, this time because of a war in Spain. The Spanish people had voted for a new government to replace the Spanish monarchy. The new democratic government was a Republic. Soon afterward, the right-wing military rose up against the government. More fighting followed as each group fought for control. A general, Francisco Franco, became the head of the opposing Nationalist government, which soon controlled all of northern Spain. Over four thousand people were massacred in a ten-day period. As a fascist dictator, Franco was supported by the Italian and German governments.

By Christmas Day in 1936, the first American soldiers left for Spain to fight with the Spanish Loyalists. The International Brigade, which included soldiers from both the United States and Canada, aided the Republican army. Less than two months later, the American Abraham Lincoln Brigade moved to the front lines, and many were killed.

Hughes was one of several writers who felt he should be present during the war in Spain. Another was Ernest Hemingway, who would write *For Whom the Bell Tolls* about the Spanish Civil War. Hughes arrived in August 1937 as a reporter for the *Baltimore Afro-American:* "And now, in Madrid, Spain's besieged capital, I've met wide-awake Negroes from various parts of the world—New York, our Middle West, the French West Indies, Cuba, Africa—some stationed here, others on leave from their battalions—all of them here because they know that if Fascism creeps across Spain, across Europe, and then across the world, there will be no more place for intelligent young Negroes at all. In fact, no decent place for any Negroes—because Fascism preaches the creed of Nordic supremacy and a world for whites alone."[7]

In 1938, the Prime Minister of the Republic announced a withdrawal of all international troops. Franco and the Nationalists captured the rest of Spain within a year. Five months later, World War II began.

One of the first things Hughes did after returning from Europe was create the Harlem Suitcase Theater. He decided it would be a theater-in-the-round, where the stage sits in the middle of the theater and is surrounded on all sides by the audience. Hughes hired Toy Harper to work on costumes. She also kept an eye on things when he wasn't around. He wrote a play that incorporated some of his poems in a theme that included blues and African American nationalism. *Don't You Want to Be Free?* opened on April 21, 1938, as a hit.

Arna Bontemps

Arna Wendell Bontemps (1902–1973) was an African American teacher, author, editor, and historian. He wrote or edited over thirty books about African American culture, including children's books and collections with Langston Hughes. The two writers became the best of friends and exchanged over 2,300 letters in their lifetime.

Born in Alexandria, Louisiana, Bontemps lived with his grandmother, as Hughes had. He moved to California at a young age. When he graduated from Pacific Union College at age seventeen, he knew he wanted to be a writer. He moved to Harlem, where other African American artists were gathering. He began by writing

Arna Bontemps

poetry, including "Nocturne at Bethesda," and won poetry contests in 1926 and 1927. Bontemps and Hughes first met during the Harlem Renaissance. One of Bontemps' first popular works was about an African American jockey. The book, *God Sends Sunday,* was later turned into a successful musical comedy for the stage called *St. Louis Woman.* For his next novel, Bontemps wrote about the Gabriel Prosser slave rebellion of 1800.

History was to remain a strong interest throughout his life. The history that fascinated him most was that of the African American people. He wrote about the fugitive slaves following the North Star to freedom and the African American migration north after World War I. In *We Have Tomorrow,* he wrote biographical sketches about African Americans and their contributions to America. His *Story of the Negro* won the Jane Addams Children's Book Award. It was also a 1949 Newbery Honor book.

Bontemps and Hughes first collaborated on a Haitian folk tale for children in 1932 called *Popo and Fifina.* Other memorable collaborations included the anthologies *The Book of Negro Folklore* (1959) and *American Negro Poetry* (1963). In the later 1930s, Bontemps and Hughes started doing a lecture tour together. They began in Illinois and traveled through the Southwest. Scheduled to speak in Denver, they were refused rooms in thirteen hotels because of their race. They enjoyed a series of talks in California schools called "How Stories and Poems Are Born" and "Making Words Sing, Talk, and Dance."

Bontemps suggested another two-month tour, which took them to Kansas City before stops in the Midwest and North.

The two friends wrote each other from 1925 until Hughes's death in 1967. Hughes looked forward to letters from his friend that often began with "Dear Lang." According to Bontemps-Hughes authority Charles H. Nichols, "Bontemps was deeply impressed by Hughes's naturalness, ease and spontaneity and by his use of blues and jazz idioms."[8]

Hughes enjoyed visiting the Bontemps family. Arna's wife, Alberta, said the two were closer than blood brothers. Although there were similarities, she saw differences in how they dressed and certain habits. Hughes drank alcohol, which her husband rarely touched. Bontemps was a voracious reader, while Hughes read little. Mrs. Bontemps enjoyed seeing Hughes with their six children. One of the children, Paul, remembered Langston as a man of laughter who never talked down to them.

Through the thirties and forties, Bontemps was a busy man. Working on a graduate degree in English at the University of Chicago, he continued to write and travel around the country giving talks. He and Hughes survived during the Depression by giving readings for as little as $25 each all over the country. Bontemps worked on a WPA volume on African Americans in Chicago. (The WPA—Work Progress Administration—was a program designed to provide some financial relief during the Depression.) After winning a Rosenwald Fellowship, he traveled to the Caribbean and wrote.

In 1940, Bontemps was appointed cultural director of the American Negro Exposition in Chicago. One of his first projects was finding a place for Hughes to live, as his friend had agreed to help by working on a book of celebrated African American musicals.

Arna Bontemps collaborated with and befriended other writers of the day also. It was he and Countee Cullen who turned *God Sends Sunday* into *St. Louis Woman*. He also befriended Richard Wright, novelist of *Native Son*.

By 1943, Bontemps started working at the college level both as professor and librarian. For more than twenty years he worked at Fisk University in Nashville. After retiring in 1966, he received two honorary degrees. He also worked at the University of Illinois and Yale University (as curator of the James Weldon Johnson Collection at the Beinecke Library) before returning to Fisk as writer-in-residence.

In 1988, fifteen years after Bontemps's death, the Arna Bontemps African American Museum and Cultural Arts Center was established in his first home in Alexandria, Louisiana. It claims to be the first African American museum in Louisiana.

Langston Hughes with one of the poets he mentored, Gwendolyn Brooks, in 1949. Brooks became the first African American to win the Pulitzer Prize in literature.

Chapter 9

The "Shakespeare of Harlem"

Hughes had a hit play, but was too distracted by his personal life to enjoy it. He had just learned that his mother's condition was getting worse. After bringing her to New York to live with him, she died on June 3, 1938. Langston had lost both of his parents within a few years of each other.

It is not known what happened to Homer Clark, but Hughes still considered stepbrother Kit his family. He had dedicated a children's poetry book, *The Dream Keeper,* to his "brother, Gwyn Clark" in 1934. Hughes paid for Kit to attend college, but Kit flunked out. Like his father, Kit drifted in and out of people's lives. He suffered from alcoholism. Possibly, Kit's entry into the army at 1942 helped, although Hughes and his stepbrother would no longer have a close relationship. Hughes did continue to have contact with Kit's children and their mother, though.

Hughes also made time to encourage young poets. In the 1930s, he met sixteen-year-old Gwendolyn Brooks while in Chicago. She demonstrated an immense amount of talent. He encouraged her to continue reading and writing. A year later, her poems were being published regularly in the *Chicago Defender* newspaper. She later became the first African American writer to win the Pulitzer Prize for literature for her second collection of poetry, *Annie Allen* (1949). With a proselike structure, the poems in *Annie Allen* tell the story of an African American woman's journey from childhood to adulthood.

Not long after his mother's funeral, which had to be paid for by Amy Spingarn due to his penniless state, Hughes returned to California, where he worked on screenplays. Again, Noel Sullivan had graciously furnished him with a place to live and work, this time at Hollow Hills Farm. Hughes finished the first volume of his autobiography, *The Big Sea*. The title came from one of the lines in the book: "Literature is a big sea full of many fish. I let down my net and pulled."[1]

Although he worked on the book in 1939, it ended in 1931, the year before his trip to the Soviet Union. There was no mention of radical beliefs or writings. Americans were becoming increasingly suspicious of the Soviets, but it was more than that. Hearing that the Soviet leader, Stalin, had signed a non-aggression pact with Hitler was upsetting. *The Big Sea* was published in 1940. It received good reviews from many publications, including the *New York Times* and *Newsweek* magazine. Yet it was largely overshadowed by a novel by another African American writer, *Native Son* by Richard Wright. *Native Son* was a monumental work that changed white readers' perceptions of African Americans. Like Hughes, Wright wrote poetry and short stories also, but it was his novels that made his name widely known. Another bestselling work was his autobiographical *Black Boy*.

With his mother's medical bills still to pay, Hughes was happy to receive a Rosenwald Fellowship in 1941, which allowed him to continue playwriting. He finally had a break when Kurt Weill and Elmer Rice chose him as the lyricist for the 1947 musical adaptation of Rice's play *Street Scene*. Critics hailed *Street Scene* as a breakthrough in American opera. Financially, *Street Scene* proved to be a breakthrough in Hughes's cycle of poverty. He was able to buy his first and only home in Harlem six months after his forty-sixth birthday. Located three blocks from Harlem's center, Hughes shared the brownstone with the Harpers.

In between writing plays, Hughes began writing his second autobiography. He wrote to Bontemps in early 1941: "But best news of all is I started my new book the other night, by accident—which is the best way to start. So the second autobiography is off to a first draft. I bought a big note book and write long hand in bed. Determined to follow your example and do FOUR pages a day, rain, sun, or landslide. . . ."[2]

Hughes's political beliefs were starting to shift. Witnessing the bravery of the American Abraham Lincoln Brigade in Spain's Civil War filled him with pride. Although he opposed war, he supported the United States when it joined World War II in 1941. At the second anniversary celebration of the United Service Organization (USO), a voluntary organization that entertained troops at Oklahoma's Fort Sill, he was thrilled that the soldiers had requested him. The

African American press took on a campaign called the Double-V, meaning victory at home and victory abroad. Hughes tried to do his part by writing jingles that persuaded people to buy war bonds. While he encouraged African Americans to support the war effort, he never lost an opportunity to remind the U.S. government that it should be providing the same freedom for *all* its citizens, just as it was fighting for these freedoms overseas.

Two collections of his poetry were published at this time, *Shakespeare in Harlem* and *Jim Crow's Last Stand.* Both strongly attacked the practice of racial segregation in the United States. Blanche Knopf worried that *Shakespeare in Harlem* might be too radical, yet Van Vechten encouraged her to publish it. *Jim Crow's Last Stand* was even stronger. Knopf didn't publish it. The Negro Publication Society of America in Atlanta published it in 1943.

In a speech given that year and later reprinted in the *Langston Hughes Reader,* Hughes said: "The American Negro believes in democracy. We want to make it real, complete, workable, not only for ourselves—the fifteen million dark ones—but for all Americans all over the land."[3]

One poem written in this time period, "Let America Be America Again" summed up the confusion of the era. Published in part in *Esquire,* the poem pleads for an America that never existed, an America for "the Negro bearing slavery's scar."

> *O, let America be America again—*
> *The land that never has been yet—*
> *And yet must be—the land where every man is free.*
> *The land that's mine—the poor man's, Indian's, Negro's, ME—*
> *Who made America,*
> *Whose sweat and blood, whose faith and pain,*
> *Whose hand at the foundry, whose plow in the rain,*
> *Must bring back our mighty dream again.*[4]

Hughes celebrated twenty years as a writer with the anniversary of the publication of *The Negro Speaks of Rivers.* Always ready for a challenge, he started writing a weekly column for the *Chicago Defender* on November 21, 1942. The *Chicago Defender* had been the most widely read African American weekly publication since World War I. The paper once billed itself as "The World's Greatest Weekly," but over time its slogan has changed to "Empowering the Community Since 1905."

Hughes earned $15 for each thousand-word column. Out of the column came a fictional character named Jesse B. Semple, who became better known as "Simple." The Harlem character sat in a neighborhood bar and addressed topics of the day. He first appeared as a character who needed to be encouraged to support a racially segregated military. People responded to Simple's philosophy. Hughes found that he enjoyed using humor to make people think about important issues. "I'm getting wonderful fan letters through my column. Three today, one from two house servants in darkest Mississippi; another from the colored sailors on a Pacific battleship,"[5] he wrote to Bontemps. The column ran for twenty years. The first of five books about Simple, *Simple Speaks His Mind*, was published in 1950. When Van Vechten reviewed it for *The New York Times*, he told Hughes: "*Simple* is a wonderful book, perhaps your most typical & best."[6]

Hughes worked on many projects at once, joking with Bontemps that he was becoming nothing more than a literary factory. In 1943, he told Bontemps, "*I Wonder As I Wander* might even now be published, if I did not wander even more than I wonder. But I expect to sit down and finish it this summer."[7] Eleven years later he still struggled with the impending deadline for his second autobiography. His intention had been to write from the massive amount of information he had saved: letters, contracts, notes. Instead, he wrote from memory as he had with *The Big Sea*.

Some of his "wandering" included the reading/book tours he continued giving. In 1945, he began another at the State Teachers College in Eau Claire, Wisconsin. After a few readings in the North, he headed to the South, finding transportation as much of a problem as ever because of the Jim Crow laws. Yet two years later, he agreed to spend a semester at Atlanta University as a creative writing professor. While there, he also taught a course called "The Negro in American Poetry."

Hughes took pleasure from writing song lyrics, most of which were for musicals. He was particularly proud of a song called "America's Young Black Joe" about boxer Joe Louis. Near the end of World War II, Hughes wrote a theme song for the Negro Freedom Rally called "For This We Fight." Songwriting didn't pay well, and Hughes kept threatening to give it up, but he often returned to writing lyrics.

As World War II ended, anti-communist hysteria swept the nation. People referred to communism as the "Red Scare" or the "Red Menace." Hughes had been on the FBI's "Key Figures" list in 1945, but the FBI decided that his communist ties were minimal. Then FBI Director J. Edgar Hoover requested that he be investigated again.

The flames of hysteria were further fanned by Wisconsin senator Joseph McCarthy, who headed an investigation that some believed was nothing more than a witch hunt. Because of Hughes's more radical work and the fact that he had lived in the Soviet Union for a year, he was summoned before a committee to answer allegations of belonging to the Communist party. He testified that he had never been a member of the Communist party. Although the committee accepted his answers, his reputation suffered. A flyer circulated with the words from "Goodbye Christ," a poem he had written during his year in the Soviet Union. Although he had supported American efforts in the Spanish Civil War and World War II, the flyer referred to him as a "Notorious Negro Stalin lover." With protesters carrying signs branding Hughes as a traitor, readings and lectures were canceled and books sales dropped.

McCarthyism

McCarthyism is a term used to describe a dark time in United States history when personal freedoms were suspended. As early as World War I, an adviser of President Woodrow Wilson spread suspicions that Soviet leaders like Trotsky and Lenin were actually German spies. Although the rumors were proved false, they were the beginning of many allegations. The Russian Revolution of 1917 brought communism to Russia, later known as the Soviet Union. After World War II, distrust grew between the United States and the Soviet Union. Communists took over the governments of China and Czechoslovakia. The Soviet Union aided North Korean communists in invading South Korea. Two very different types of governments (democratic and communist) each competed to be the stronger world power. Weapons technology led to whispers of atomic and

Joseph McCarthy

nuclear weapons beings launched. This period in history is known as the Cold War, a time when Americans feared communism, and Russians feared democracy.

A Communist political party started in the United States. In many cases, members had close ties to the labor movement, which organized unions at places of employment. The U.S. House of Representatives created the House Un-American Activities Committee to investigate charges of disloyalty. By the 1950s, President Harry S Truman established loyalty boards to investigate federal employees. If anyone's loyalty to America was questioned, they were fired. One employee for the State Department, Alger Hiss, was accused of giving government secrets to the Soviet Union. He was convicted of perjury and imprisoned. He spent the rest of his life unsuccessfully trying to clear his name. An American couple, Julius and Ethel Rosenberg, were convicted and executed for being Soviet spies. They both proclaimed their innocence to the end. Government documents released in 1995 showed that Julius Rosenberg was a spy, but there was never any definitive proof that his wife was.

In 1950, a senator named Joseph McCarthy began making accusations that many problems in the United States were the result of communism and that some government leaders were actually communists. In a telegram to President Truman on February 11, Senator McCarthy stated that he had the names of fifty-seven communists working in the State Department, and he knew that there were many more. He wrote: "The day the House Un-American Activities committee exposed Alger Hiss as an important link in an Inter-National Communist Spy Ring, you signed an order forbidding the State Departments giving to the Congress any information in regard to the disloyalty or the Communistic connections of anyone in that department, despite this State Department blackout, we have been able to compile a list of 57 Communists in the State Department."[8]

McCarthy demanded that the President turn over all names of employees placed by Hiss and anyone else with communist ties. Not doing so, McCarthy stated, would show that the Democratic Party was working with the Communist Party.

No truth was ever found in McCarthy's charges, but he continued making accusations of Communist Party members or communist sympathizers in the United States. McCarthy investigated professionals including writers, directors, actors, clergymen, journalists, and college professors. *McCarthyism* became a term used to describe widespread public accusations of disloyalty to the United States. People accused of Communist sympathies were often blacklisted and unable to find work. Writers like Hughes protested the banning of books and censorship McCarthyism caused.

By 1954, the hysteria from McCarthyism began to die down. Yet by that time, many careers and lives had been destroyed. The following year, the United States Senate condemned Joseph McCarthy for conduct unbecoming to a senator. The Supreme Court ruled on cases in following years that would protect an individual's rights against such accusations.

Langston Hughes stands in front of his house in Harlem in 1962. When not traveling, he spent the last twenty-five years of his life in Harlem, the place he considered home.

Chapter 10

"A Dream Deferred"

Soon after Hughes was questioned by the McCarthy committee, Joseph McCarthy was discredited. With a renewed sense of purpose, Hughes finished writing about his year in the Soviet Union for his second autobiography, *I Wonder as I Wander*. Published in 1956, most people agreed it was much more personal than *The Big Sea*. Van Vechten again reviewed his friend's work and told him that he enjoyed the Russian section the most.

For the last twenty-five years of his life, Hughes lived in his beloved Harlem when he wasn't traveling. The people of Harlem were his extended family, particularly Toy and Emerson Harper. After living in poverty most of his life, Hughes began to see moderate financial success from his efforts. Yet he continued the frenetic pace he had begun in the early fifties. He began writing more for children, from books of poetry to history. Particularly successful was a series of five "First" books that began with *The First Book of Negroes* in 1952 and ended with *The First Book of Africa* in 1960. This led to a series of "Famous" books that includes *Famous American Negroes* and *Famous Negro Music Makers*. African American children had grown up reading about famous white people and famous white history. Hughes wanted children to know there was African American history.

Hughes continued his involvement in the theater during the 1960s. A play based on his *Shakespeare in Harlem* poetry collection debuted, using four or five vignettes of people in the bars and tenements. *The New York Times* said of the play, "But the poet of Harlem is probably the man who has the most affectionate understanding of his neighbors. He enjoys being one of them. He sees the humor as well as the misery of their experience."[1]

Hughes also began working for television. He found that the growing medium provided another avenue for bringing music to people. His renewed interest in gospel music led to a Christmas show called *Black Nativity* (1961) and later *Jericho—Jim Crow* (1964). Hughes recorded some of his poetry accompanied by blues and jazz music. He wrote: "Jazz to me is one of the inherent expressions of Negro life in America: the eternal beating in the Negro soul."[2] Hundreds of his poems have been set to music. He read some of his earlier verse accompanied by jazz great Charles Mingus in *Ask Your Mama: 12 Moods for Jazz*. He wasn't the only one who read poetry set to music, either. Carl Sandburg gave readings on television on the show *Poetry with Jazz*.

Hughes worked on a successful movie, *Raisin in the Sun,* based on a play by Lorraine Hansberry and starring Sidney Poitier. The title of the play and movie came from a Hughes poem called "Harlem" and later renamed "Dream Deferred." The poem asks: "What happens to a dream deferred? Does it dry up like a raisin in the sun?"[3]

Hughes published collections of poetry, short stories, and anthologies. Some of his plays were published as *Five Plays by Langston Hughes*. Other collections include *The Ballad of the Brown King* (1961), *Something in Common and Other Stories* (1963), and *Simple's Uncle Sam* (1965). *Ask Your Mama* (1961) was dedicated to "Louis Armstrong, the greatest horn blower of them all."[4]

As Hughes grew older, history took on greater importance. He wrote the text for a pictorial history of the African American in the United States by photographer Roy DeCarava, *The Sweet Flypaper of Life*. He wrote a history of the NAACP, *Fight for Freedom,* in 1962.

Hughes further broke down walls of discrimination by becoming the first African American to be admitted to the international writers' organization known as PEN. A longtime friend of the Spingarn family, he was particularly honored to win the 45th annual Spingarn Award, the NAACP's highest honor for achievement among African Americans. He was also inducted into the National Institute of Arts and Letters, one of the highest honors for an American writer. In 1961, he was only the second African American ever to receive this honor.

Hughes made at least eight extensive cross-country tours in his lifetime, talking to everyone from kindergarteners to soldiers. Often he spoke at schools, but he also spoke at reform schools and prisons. Hughes traveled in Europe and

Africa as a sort of goodwill ambassador during the 1960s. In December 1961, he was one of thirty-three African American artists, performers, and educators who took park in a cultural exchange program in Lagos, Nigeria. The following year, while attending a writer's conference in Africa, he dedicated an American library in Ghana and presented *Black Nativity* at a festival in Italy. Hughes was also acknowledged as a historic artistic figure at the First World Festival of Negro Arts in Dakar, Senegal, in 1966.

Hughes moved his weekly newspaper column from the *Chicago Defender* to the more prestigious *New York Post*. He continued to use his column to push causes important to him. One of these was recognition of his good friend, Arna Bontemps. "The distinguished author and Librarian of Fisk University has long been an outstanding contributor of the American literary scene as well as to the field of national scholarship. He is an authority on Negro life, literature and folk lore,"[5] he wrote. Hughes's character, Simple, didn't transition well to the 1960s. In 1965, when African Americans accused Hughes of making fun of racial problems, he stopped writing the column.

As the civil rights movement gained strength, Hughes worried about the increasing militancy in the Black Power movement. Black Power started as a political group advocating racial pride and independence. Some factions promoted violence against white people. After his nephew joined a militant group and was found murdered, Hughes began defending more conservative activists such as educator Booker T. Washington. As a young adult, Hughes had found Washington's philosophy of education and improving life through learning a trade both simplistic and oppressive. He now saw Washington as another voice in the long journey toward freedom that African Americans had made. He recalled his grandmother taking him to hear Washington speak before a packed auditorium at the University of Kansas. Hughes wrote "Ballad of Booker T" in tribute of the man. He began the poem:

> *Booker T.*
> *Was a practical man.*
> *He said, Till the soil*
> *And learn from the land.*

He made peace with any disagreements he had felt toward Washington by writing:

He started out
In a simple way—
For yesterday
Was not today.[6]

Hughes found it amusing that suddenly people wanted to write about him. Within a month in 1962, five people approached him about writing books about his life. Hughes preferred that Bontemps write the story of his life, but Bontemps died in 1973 before doing so.

In 1963 at the age of sixty-one, Hughes began thinking about the end of his life. He wrote a will deciding who would receive what copyrights to his work. At the urging of Carl Van Vechten, he organized the letters he had exchanged with friends and peers over the years and donated the letters to Yale. Charles H. Nichols, an authority on African American literature, stated that the letters between Hughes and Bontemps were especially significant in their chronicling of African American culture and a great friendship. "Their association was fruitful and mutually satisfying. And their work is clearly related to a number of significant developments in our recent literature."[7]

Early in May 1967, Hughes experienced severe abdominal pain and was admitted to New York Polyclinic Hospital. It is unclear whether his doctors knew who he was, as he signed in as "James L. Hughes." Only his secretary and Arna Bontemps knew of his admission at the beginning. An infection followed prostate surgery. Hughes died on May 22 from septic shock. His memorial service included the playing of a blues song written by Duke Ellington, "Do Nothing Till You Hear from Me," and a few words by Bontemps. Later, a smaller group gathered for the cremation. As the body was wheeled off, the mourners held hands and recited "The Negro Speaks of Rivers." In his obituary of May 23, 1967, *The New York Times* referred to him as the "O. Henry of Harlem," comparing his published work to the productive short story writer of the early twentieth century.

Hughes's work continued to be published over the following year. *The New York Times* had this to say about Langston Hughes: "After the bulk of his work has had a chance to shake down, he will be recognized for what he was: an American writer of charm and vitality whose outgoing manner did not hide the weight of argument behind it."[8]

The influence of the civil rights movement was seen in a poetry collection titled *The Panther and the Lash,* which was published soon after his death. He had dedicated it to Rosa Parks, who had been the spark for the 1955 Montgomery bus boycott. Collaborations such as *Black Magic* (with Milton Meltzer, 1967) and a revision of the 1949 anthology *The Poetry of the Negro 1746–1970* (edited by Hughes and Bontemps) were also published.

In the 1970s, *Good Morning Revolution*, a collection of Hughes's radical verse and essays, was released. Faith Berry, editor of the volume and authority on Hughes, believed it was some of his best work. Arnold Rampersad helped gather and edit *Collected Poems*, a comprehensive and well-indexed chronological collection of his poetry, published in 1994.

Hughes's amazing body of work has been translated into every major language, including French, Italian, Spanish, Swedish, Chinese, Russian, and Japanese. It includes forty-six books, eight edited works, over twenty plays, and countless song lyrics. Hughes influenced and helped many notable writers over the years. He published a young woman's first short story in *The Best Short Stories by Negro Writers* (1967). The woman, Alice Walker, later went on to receive the Pulitzer Prize for *The Color Purple,* which also became a major motion picture.

In the Queens Borough Public Library system, the Langston Hughes Community Library and Cultural Center opened in 1969, making it the first public facility named after the poet and writer. The New York City Preservation Commission gave landmark status to Hughes's home at 20 East 127th Street in Harlem. In 1991, the Pinckney School in Lawrence, Kansas, where he attended second grade, named its library The Langston Hughes Library for Children.

On the eighty-ninth anniversary of his birth in 1991, Hughes's cremated remains were interred beneath the commemoratively designed "I've Known Rivers" tile floor in the Schomburg Center for Research in Black Culture in the Harlem branch of the New York Public Library. Today, visitors to the research center may see this floor and remember the man. The Langston Hughes Collections at the Schomburg Center include foreign language translations of his work in addition to autographed manuscripts, drafts of poems; scripts for radio, motion pictures, and television; Broadway revues and musicals; playbills; photographs; and audio recordings.

Langston Hughes is one of America's greatest poets. Throughout his long career, he believed that art should be accessible to as many people as possible. His racial pride was evident in his body of work, and he used his art to communicate his feelings about politics and injustice. Often, he struggled with what he wanted to write and what his audience expected. He did his best to deliver what would satisfy both. Hughes wrote about what he knew—the people, places, and events around him. He has earned the often used title of African American Poet Laureate.

The Civil Rights Movement

By the middle of the twentieth century, increasing attention focused on discrimination against African American people. A seamstress and activist named Rosa Parks got on a Montgomery, Alabama, bus one day in 1955. When she refused to give up her bus seat to a white person, she was arrested for violating a city law that stated African Americans must give up their seats for white people who wanted them. Montgomery African Americans organized a protest to boycott city transportation. The next day, African Americans walked, carpooled, bicycled, and even road mules. The bus line came to a standstill. After 382 days and still no African American ridership, the city abolished the law.

Rosa Parks

The Montgomery bus boycott was the beginning of many protests against discrimination and segregation. Parks spent the rest of her life as an activist and is referred to as the "mother of the civil rights movement."

When the United States Supreme Court declared in 1954 that public school segregation was illegal, some schools had to be forced to desegregate. Two well-known cases involved an Arkansas high school and a Mississippi university. In 1957, nine African American children were to be admitted to Central High in Little Rock, Arkansas. It took several attempts and the assistance of federal troops ordered by President Dwight D. Eisenhower for the children to finally be allowed to enter the school.

When James Meredith applied for admission to the University of Mississippi in 1961, he wasn't the first African American to be turned down. On May 31 of that year, the NAACP Legal Defense and Educational Fund filed suit on Meredith's behalf in the U.S. District Court. They alleged that Meredith was being denied admission to the University of Mississippi based solely on his race. The United States Supreme Court agreed and ruled that he should be admitted. However, Mississippi governor Ross Barnett publicly stated that he would block Meredith's entrance. After U.S. Attorney General Robert Kennedy arranged for Meredith to be registered, the young man was escorted to campus where federal marshals, U.S. border patrol, and federal prison guards would protect him. Two thousand people gathered, throwing things and assaulting the guards. It took additional federal troops to regain order. Two people died and almost two hundred were injured on both sides at the University of Mississippi that day. Despite the violence, Meredith did attend the university; he graduated in 1964.

One of the leaders of the civil rights movement was the Reverend Martin Luther King Jr., who urged peaceful protests—sit-ins, boycotts, and marches. In 1957, King and other Southern clergymen formed the Southern Christian Leadership Conference (SCLC) to coordinate the work of civil rights groups. Three years later, they were joined by college students from the Student Nonviolent Coordinating Committee (SNCC). Together, these groups stopped discrimination in many public places. Still, discrimination continued in other areas. Many people urged the government to pass federal laws making discrimination illegal. More than 200,000 people took part in the March on Washington in August 1963 to gain the attention of the government. It was there that Dr. King gave his famous "I Have a Dream" speech. After the march, President John F. Kennedy pushed for stronger laws to stop discrimination, but he was assassinated three months later. One of the things that President Lyndon Johnson, who followed Kennedy, did after taking office was to convince Congress to pass the Civil Rights Act of 1964. The act prohibited discrimination in public places and stated that there should be equal opportunities in jobs and schools regardless of race, color, religion, or national origin.

In the South, many elected officials refused to enforce the federal laws that gave African Americans equality. One of these was the right to vote. Many protests about voting rights resulted in the deaths of those who worked toward it. In 1965, Congress passed the Voting Rights Act.

Rioting broke out after the assassination of the Reverend King in 1968. Many of these riots were in urban areas where poor African Americans lived in substandard conditions in ghettos. President Johnson urged Congress to approve the Civil Rights Act of 1968, also known as the Fair Housing Act, which prohibited racial discrimination in the sale and rental of housing.

Monitoring civil rights is an ongoing process for the United States. Parents and teachers educate children about equality. Organizations like the NAACP serve as watchdogs to alert people to problems. The legal system enforces the principles of equality for everyone. Like the United States government, civil rights depends on a system of checks and balances.

Chronology

1902	James Langston Hughes is born in Joplin, Missouri, on February 1; his father leaves for Mexico later that year
1914	Grandmother Mary Langston dies; mother (Carrie Langston Hughes) remarries; Langston moves from Lawrence to live with mother, stepfather, and stepbrother in Lincoln, Illinois
1916	Is elected class poet at graduation in Lincoln; moves from Lincoln to Cleveland, Ohio
1919	Spends the summer with father in Mexico
1920	Is chosen editor of Central High School Yearbook, Cleveland; graduates from Central High School and goes back to Mexico
1921	Publishes works for children in *The Brownies' Book;* "A Negro Speaks of Rivers" is published in *The Crisis;* enters Columbia University in New York
1922	Leaves Columbia to take assorted jobs in New York area
1923	Works on ships that sail to Africa and Europe
1924	Is employed as cook in a Paris nightclub; returns from Europe to live with his mother in Washington, D.C.
1925	Wins first prize for poetry in *Opportunity* contest; meets Carl Van Vechten, who introduces his poetry to Blanche Knopf of Knopf Publishing House
1926	Enters Lincoln University in Pennsylvania; *Weary Blues* is published
1927	Second book of poetry, *Fine Clothes to the Jew,* is published; Charlotte Mason becomes his patron
1929	Graduates from Lincoln University
1930	First novel, *Not Without Laughter,* is published; wins William E. Harmon Award for literature; travels to Cuba; Mrs. Mason ends her patronage
1931	Conducts poetry reading tour in the heavily discriminatory South and West of the United States; visits Cuba and Haiti with Zell Ingram
1932	Travels to Russia
1933	Returns from Russia; spends year writing at Carmel-by-the-Sea
1934	*Ways of White Folks* is published
1935	Receives Guggenheim Fellowship
1937	Travels to Spain as correspondent for *Baltimore Afro-American*
1938	*Don't You Want to Be Free?* opens in Hughes's Harlem Suitcase Theater; mother dies

1940	*The Big Sea* is published
1942	*Shakespeare in Harlem* is published; begins weekly column for *Chicago Defender*
1947–1948	Is appointed Visiting Professor of Creative Writing at Atlanta University
1950	*Simple Speaks His Mind* is published
1951	*Montage on a Dream Deferred* is published
1956	*I Wonder As I Wander* is published
1960	Receives Spingarn Medal
1961	Inducted into the National Institute of Arts and Letters
1963	*Five Plays* is published
1967	Dies on May 22
1991	His cremated remains are interred beneath the commemoratively designed "I've Known Rivers" tile floor in the Schomburg Center for Research in Black Culture in Harlem

Selected Works

Poetry
The Weary Blues
Fine Clothes to the Jew
The Negro Mother and Other Dramatic Recitations
Dear Lovely Death
The Dream Keeper and Other Poems
Scottsboro Limited: Four Poems and a Play
A New Song
Shakespeare in Harlem
Jim Crow's Last Stand
Freedom's Plow
Fields of Wonder
One-Way Ticket
Montage of a Dream Deferred
The Panther and the Lash: Poems of Our Times
The Collected Poems of Langston Hughes
The Block: Poems
Carol of the Brown King: Poems
The Pasteboard Bandit

Fiction

Not Without Laughter
The Ways of White Folks
Simple Speaks His Mind
Laughing to Keep from Crying
Simple Takes a Wife
Simple Stakes a Claim
Tambourines to Glory
Something in Common and Other Stories
Simple's Uncle Sam
The Return of Simple
Short Stories of Langston Hughes

Nonfiction

The Big Sea: An Autobiography
The Sweet Flypaper of Life (with Roy De Carava)
I Wonder as I Wander: An Autobiographical Journey
A Pictorial History of the Negro in America (with Milton Meltzer)
Fight for Freedom: The Story of the NAACP
Black Misery

Other

Ask Your Mama: 12 Moods for Jazz
The Langston Hughes Reader
Simply Heavenly (book and lyrics by Hughes, music by David Martin)
The Ballad of the Brown King (libretto by Hughes, music by Margaret Bonds)
Good Morning Revolution: Uncollected Social Protest Writings by Langston Hughes

Children's Books

The Block: Poems
Carol of the Brown King: Nativity Poems
Don't You Turn Back: Poems
The Dream Keeper and Other Poems
Famous American Negroes
The First Book of Jazz
The First Book of Negroes
The First Book of Rhythms
The First Book of the West Indies
The First Book of Africa
The Langston Hughes Reader
The Pasteboard Bandit (with Arna Bontemps)
Popo and Fifina: Children of Haiti (with Arna Bontemps)
The Sweet and Sour Animal Book

Timeline in History

1857	The U.S. Supreme Court upholds slavery in the Dred Scott decision.

1857 The U.S. Supreme Court upholds slavery in the Dred Scott decision.

1861 The Civil War begins.

1865 The Emancipation Proclamation frees slaves in America. The Civil War ends. Abraham Lincoln is assassinated.

1903 Orville and Wilbur Wright fly the first mechanically propelled airplane.

1909 The National Association for the Advancement of Colored People (NAACP) is formed on February 12 by people working for equality and social justice.

1917 The U.S. enters World War I. The Russian Revolution introduces a socialist government and forms the Soviet Union.

1918 World War I ends.

1919 Mohandas Gandhi begins nonviolent reform movement in India.

1929 The U.S. stock market crashes, leading to the Great Depression.

1933 President Franklin Roosevelt introduces "New Deal" reforms to solve the economic and unemployment problems brought on by the Depression.

1935 The University of Maryland Law School is forced to admit an African American student.

1939 World War II begins in Europe.

1941 The Japanese bomb Pearl Harbor and the United States enters the war; President Franklin Roosevelt signs nondiscrimination policy in employment with the federal government and defense industries.

1945 World War II ends; United Nations is formed.

1947 Jackie Robinson joins the Dodgers, breaking the color barrier in Major League Baseball.

1948 U.S. armed forces are racially integrated.

1950 McCarthyism begins as Senator Joe McCarthy holds hearings attacking suspected communists.

1954 Landmark case *Brown vs. Board of Education* makes segregation in schools illegal.

1955 Rosa Parks refuses to give up her seat on a Montgomery, Alabama, bus, leading to a yearlong boycott of buses until segregation on buses is made illegal.

1957 Federal troops are sent in to protect and escort nine African American students to Little Rock High School.

1960	Four African American students stage a sit-in at a Greensboro, North Carolina, lunch counter. Other peaceful demonstrations are held in Southern cities to protest segregation at eating establishments.
1961	Volunteers called Freedom Riders bring attention to segregated public transportation and public facilities.
1962	Federal troops must be called in to escort African American student James Meredith to the University of Mississippi.
1963	March on Washington is held in Washington, D.C., as 250,000 people march for equality; Martin Luther King Jr. delivers his "I Have a Dream" speech; President John F. Kennedy is assassinated.
1964	Civil Rights Act is passed, making discrimination in employment, housing, and public facilities illegal.
1965	Voting Rights Act is passed, which stops unfair requirements that prohibit voter registration. U.S. troops are sent to Vietnam. Racial riots occur in many urban areas.
1967	Thurgood Marshall becomes the first African American Supreme Court justice.
1968	Martin Luther King Jr. is assassinated in Memphis, Tennessee.
1969	Neil Armstrong becomes the first human to walk on the moon.
1973	U.S. withdraws troops from Vietnam.
1981	NAACP pushes for Voting Rights Act to be extended for 25 years. The following year, voter registration drives result in signing more than 850,000 voters. The AIDS virus is identified.
1984 & 1988	Jesse Jackson runs for the Democratic presidential nomination.
1991	The Soviet Union (U.S.S.R.) dissolves.
2000	Unprecedented results in presidential election between Al Gore and George W. Bush lead to recounting of votes and court hearings before George W. Bush is declared the winner.
2001	Civil rights groups file suit in Florida against discriminatory voting practices, such as African American voters being turned away at the polls. Terrorists crash airplanes into Pentagon and World Trade Center.
2003	President George W. Bush sends troops to invade Iraq.
2005	Hurricane Katrina strikes the Gulf Coast. Many claim rescue response time in New Orleans was slow because many of the storm's victims were black.
2006	The Supreme Court revisits the question of whether race-based admission policies, designed to achieve racial balance in schools, is constitutional.

Chapter Notes

Chapter 1
"The Weary Blues"

1. Arnold Rampersad, *The Life of Langston Hughes: Volume 1: 1902–1941; I, Too, Sing America* (New York: Oxford University Press, 1986), p. 107.

2. Langston Hughes, *Selected Poems* (New York: Vintage Books, 1959), p. 33.

3. Charles H. Nichols (editor), *Arna Bontemps—Langston Hughes Letters 1925–1967* (New York: Dodd, Mead & Company, 1980), p. 8.

4. Langston Hughes, *Langston Hughes Reader* (New York: George Brazelle, Inc., 1958), p. 335.

Chapter 2
Growing Up in Kansas

1. Faith Berry, *Langston Hughes: Before and Beyond Harlem* (Westport, Connecticut: Lawrence Hill & Company, 1983), p. 19.

2. Langston Hughes, *The Big Sea* (New York: Thunder's Mouth Press, 1956), p. 26.

3. Ibid., p. 14.

4. Ibid., p. 14.

5. Langston Hughes, *Langston Hughes Reader* (New York: George Brazelle, Inc., 1958), p. 490.

6. Hughes, *The Big Sea*, p. 12.

7. "Charles Langston's Speech at the Cuyahoga County Courthouse" Oberlin University, http://www.oberlin.edu/external/EOG/Oberlin-Wellington_Rescue/c._langston_speech.htm

8. Arnold Rampersad, *The Life of Langston Hughes: Volume 1: 1902–1941; I, Too, Sing America* (New York: Oxford University Press, 1986), p. 7.

9. Ibid., p. 13.

10. Hughes, *The Big Sea*, p. 16.

11. Berry, p. 147.

12. "Notable People: John Brown," National Park Service: *Harpers Ferry National Historic Park,* http://www.nps.gov/hafe/people.htm

Chapter 3
Northern Migration

1. Arnold Rampersad, *The Life of Langston Hughes: Volume 1: 1902–1941; I, Too, Sing America* (New York: Oxford University Press, 1986), p. 53.

2. Langston Hughes, *The Big Sea* (New York: Thunder's Mouth Press, 1956), p. 18.

3. Ibid., p. 23.

4. Ibid., p. 24.

5. Rampersad, p. 24.

6. Hughes, *The Big Sea*, p. 28.

7. Langston Hughes, *I Wonder as I Wander* (New York: Thunder's Mouth Press, 1956), p. 308.

8. Langston Hughes, *Langston Hughes Reader* (New York: George Brazelle, Inc., 1958), p. 455.

9. Hughes, *The Big Sea*, p. 35.

10. Ibid., p. 40.

11. Ibid., p. 49.

12. Ibid., p. 39.

13. Langston Hughes, *Selected Poems* (New York: Vintage Books, 1959), p. 68.

14. Hughes, *Langston Hughes Reader*, p. 491.

15. Walt Whitman, *Leaves of Grass and Selected Prose* (New York: The Modern Library, 1950), p. 267.

Chapter 4
"I've Known Rivers"

1. Langston Hughes, *The Big Sea* (New York: Thunder's Mouth Press, 1956), p. 54.

2. Langston Hughes, *Langston Hughes Reader* (New York: George Brazelle, Inc., 1958), p. 58.

3. Hughes, *The Big Sea*, p. 61.

4. Ibid., p. 70.

5. Ibid., p. 72.

6. Ibid., p. 80.

7. Ibid., p. 81.

8. Ibid., p. 96.

9. "Amendment XIV, Constitution of the United States" Charters of Freedom, http://www.archives.gov/national-archives-experience/charters/constitution_amendments_11-27.html

10. "Vision Statement" National Association for the Advancement of Colored People, http://www.naacp.org/about/about_mission.html

Chapter 5
Sailing to Africa

1. Langston Hughes, *The Big Sea* (New York: Thunder's Mouth Press, 1956), p. 3.

2. Ibid., p. 102.

3. Ibid., p. 120.

4. Arnold Rampersad, *The Life of Langston Hughes: Volume 1: 1902–1941; I, Too, Sing America* (New York: Oxford University Press, 1986), p. 63.

5. Hughes, p. 143.

6. Ibid., p. 201.

7. Emily Bernard (editor), *Remember Me to Harlem: The Letters of Langston Hughes and Carl Van Vechten, 1925–1964* (New York: Alfred A. Knopf, 2001), pp. xiii–xiv.

8. Ibid., p. 8.

9. Ibid., p. 329.

Chapter 6
Poet and Student

1. Arnold Rampersad, *The Life of Langston Hughes: Volume 1: 1902–1941; I, Too, Sing America* (New York: Oxford University Press, 1986), p. 99.

2. Langston Hughes, *The Big Sea* (New York: Thunder's Mouth Press, 1956), pp. 216–217.

3. Emily Bernard (editor), *Remember Me to Harlem: The Letters of Langston Hughes and Carl Van Vechten, 1925–1964* (New York: Alfred A. Knopf, 2001), p. 12.

4. Ibid., p. 74.

5. Alfred Kreymborg, "Five Silhouettes on the Slope of Mount Parnassus . . . The Weary Blues" *The New York Times,* March 21, 1926, p. BR6.

6. Langston Hughes, *Langston Hughes Reader* (New York: George Brazelle, Inc., 1958), p. 33.

7. Faith Berry, *Langston Hughes: Before and Beyond Harlem* (Westport, Connecticut: Lawrence Hill & Company, 1983), p. 78.

8. Hughes, *The Big Sea*, pp. 263–264.

9. Berry, p. 107.

10. Bernard, p. 74.

11. Langston Hughes, *I Wonder as I Wander* (New York: Thunder's Mouth Press, 1956), p. 4.

12. Hughes, *Langston Hughes Reader*, p. 212.

Chapter 7
Speaking to the South

1. Langston Hughes, *The Big Sea* (New York: Thunder's Mouth Press, 1956), p. 334.

2. Langston Hughes, *I Wonder as I Wander* (New York: Thunder's Mouth Press, 1956), p. 28.

3. Arnold Rampersad, *The Life of Langston Hughes: Volume 1: 1902–1941; I, Too, Sing America* (New York: Oxford University Press, 1986), p. 214.

4. Arnold Rampersad (editor), *The Collected Works of Langston Hughes: The Poems, 1921–1940, Volume 1* (Columbia, MO: Columbia University Press, 2001), p. 155.

5. Hughes, *I Wonder as I Wander*, p. 6.

6. Charles H. Nichols (editor), *Arna Bontemps–Langston Hughes Letters 1925–1967* (New York: Dodd, Mead & Company, 1980) p. 164.

7. Hughes, *I Wonder as I Wander*, p. 46.

Chapter 8
War and Death

1. Arnold Rampersad, *The Life of Langston Hughes: Volume 1: 1902–1941; I, Too, Sing America* (New York: Oxford University Press, 1986), p. 227.

2. Langston Hughes, *I Wonder as I Wander* (New York: Thunder's Mouth Press, 1956), p. 65.

3. Ibid., p. 74.

4. Rampersad, p. 252.

5. Ibid., pp. 268–269.

6. Charles H. Nichols (editor), *Arna Bontemps—Langston Hughes Letters 1925–1967* (New York: Dodd, Mead & Company, 1980), p. 39.

7. "Negroes in Spain, from The Volunteer for Liberty (1937)," Department of English, University of Illinois at Urbana-Champaign: *Modern American Poetry* http://www.english.uiuc.edu/maps/poets/g_l/hughes/inspain.htm

8. Nichols, p. 164.

Chapter 9
The "Shakespeare of Harlem"

1. Langston Hughes, *The Big Sea* (New York: Thunder's Mouth Press, 1956), p. 335.

2. Charles H. Nichols (editor), *Arna Bontemps—Langston Hughes Letters 1925–1967* (New York: Dodd, Mead & Company, 1980) p. 73.

3. Langston Hughes, *Langston Hughes Reader* (New York: George Brazelle, Inc., 1958), p. 501.

4. Arnold Rampersad (editor), *The Collected Poems of Langston Hughes* (New York: Knopf, 1994), p. 189.

5. Nichols, p. 133.

6. Emily Bernard (editor), *Remember Me to Harlem: The Letters of Langston Hughes and Carl Van Vechten, 1925–1964* (New York: Alfred A. Knopf, 2001), p. 267.

7. Nichols, p. 127.

8. "Teaching With Documents: Telegram from Senator Joseph McCarthy to President Harry S Truman," The U.S. National Archives and Records Administration, http://www.archives.gov/education/lessons/mccarthy-telegram/images/telegram-page-3.gif

Chapter 10
"A Dream Deferred"

1. "Shakespeare of Harlem" *New York Times*, February 10, 1960, p. 43.

2. Langston Hughes, *Langston Hughes Reader* (New York: George Brazelle, Inc., 1958), p. 34.

3. Ibid., p. 89.

4. Arnold Rampersad (editor), *The Collected Works of Langston Hughes: The Poems, 1921–1940, Volume 1* (Columbia, MO: Columbia University Press, 2001), p. 83.

5. Charles H. Nichols (editor), *Arna Bontemps—Langston Hughes Letters 1925–1967* (New York: Dodd, Mead & Company, 1980), p. 423.

6. Rampersad, p. 441.

7. Nichols, p. 489.

8. "Langson Hughes Dies" *New York Times*, May 24, 1967, p. 32.

Further Reading

For Young Adults

Hill, Laban Carrick. *Harlem Stomp!* New York: Little, Brown and Company, 2003.

Hughes, Langston. *The Dream Keeper and Other Poems.* New York: Knopf Books for Young Readers, 1996.

———. *Famous American Negroes.* New York: Dodd, Mead and Company, 1964.

———. *Famous Negro Heroes of America.* New York: Dodd, Mead and Company, 1962.

———. *The First Book of Africa.* New York: Franklin Watts, 1960.

———. *The First Book of Jazz.* New York: Franklin Watts, 1955.

———. *The First Book of Rhythms.* New York: Oxford University Press, 2005.

Hughes, Langston, and Arno Bontemps. *Popo and Fifina: Children of Haiti.* New York: Oxford University Press, 2005.

Hughes, Langston, Milton Meltzer, and C. Eric Lincoln. *A Pictorial History of Black Americans.* New York: Crown Publishers, Inc., 1956; reprinted 1983.

Johnson, Dianne (editor). *The Collected Works of Langston Hughes: Works for Children and Young Adults: Poetry, Fiction, and Other Writing* (Volume 11). Columbia, MO: Columbia University Press, 2003.

Leach, Laurie F. *Langston Hughes: A Biography.* Westport, CT: Greenwood Press, 2004.

Osofsky, Audrey. *Free to Dream: The Making of a Poet, Langston Hughes.* New York: Lothrop, Lee & Shepard Books, 1996.

Rampersad, Arnold (editor). *The Collected Poems of Langston Hughes.* New York: Knopf, 1994.

Walker, Alice. *Langston Hughes, American Poet.* New York: Thomas J. Crowell Co., 1974.

Works Consulted

Bernard, Emily (editor). *Remember Me to Harlem: The Letters of Langston Hughes and Carl Van Vechten, 1925–1964.* New York: Alfred A. Knopf, 2001.

Berry, Faith. *Langston Hughes: Before and Beyond Harlem.* Westport, CT: Lawrence Hill & Company, 1983.

DeSantis, Christopher C. (editor). *The Collected Works of Langston Hughes: Essays on Art, Race, Politics, and World Affairs* (Volume 9). Columbia, MO: Columbia University Press, 2002.

Domner, Dennis, and Barbara Watkins (editors) *Embattled Lawrence: Conflict and Community*. Lawrence, KS: University of Kansas Continuing Education, 2001.

Hughes, Langston. *The Big Sea*. New York: Thunder's Mouth Press, 1956.

———. *I Wonder as I Wander: An Autobiographical Journey*. New York: Thunder's Mouth Press, 1956.

———. *Langston Hughes Reader*. New York: George Brazelle, Inc., 1958.

———. *Selected Poems*. New York: New York: Vintage Books, 1959.

Miller, R. Baxter. *Langston Hughes and Gwendolyn Brooks: A Reference Guide*. Boston: G.K. Hale & Co., 1978.

Miller, R. Baxter (editor). *The Collected Works of Langston Hughes: The Short Stories* (Volume 15). Columbia, MO: Columbia University Press, 2001.

Mullen, Edward J. (editor). *Langston Hughes in the Hispanic World and Haiti*. Hamden, CT: The Shoe String Press, Inc., 1977.

Nichols, Charles H. (editor). *Arna Bontemps—Langston Hughes Letters 1925–1967*. New York: Dodd, Mead & Company, 1980.

Rampersad, Arnold (editor). *The Collected Works of Langston Hughes: The Poems, 1921–1940* (Volume 1). Columbia, MO: Columbia University Press, 2001.

———. *The Collected Works of Langston Hughes: The Poems, 1951–1967* (Volume 3). Columbia, MO: Columbia University Press, 2001.

———. *The Life of Langston Hughes: Volume 1: 1902–1941; I, Too, Sing America*. New York: Oxford University Press, 1986.

———. *The Life of Langston Hughes: Volume II: 1941–1967; I Dream A World*. New York: Oxford University Press, 1988.

Tracy, Steven C. *Langston Hughes & The Blues*. Urbana: University of Illinois Press, 1988.

Watson, Steven. *The Harlem Renaissance*. New York: Pantheon Books, 1995.

On the Internet

Academy of American Poets: *Langston Hughes*
    http://www.poets.org/poet.php/prmPID/83

Arna Bontemps African American Museum: *The Man & His Works*
    http://www.arnabontempsmuseum.com

The Blues Foundation: *What Is the Blues?*
    http://www.blues.org

Department of English, University of Illinois at Urbana-Champaign: *Modern American Poetry*, "Langston Hughes"
    http://www.english.uiuc.edu/maps/poets/g_l/hughes/hughes.htm
James Madison University: *Langston Hughes (1902–1967)* "Teacher Resource File"
    http://falcon.jmu.edu/~ramseyil/hughes.htm
Library of Congress: American Memory, "Langston Hughes"
    http://lcweb2.loc.gov/ammem/today/feb01.html
University of Missouri-Kansas City School of Law: *Famous American Trials* "The Scottsboro Boys Trials"
    http://www.law.umkc.edu/faculty/projects/FTrials/scottsboro/scottsb.htm

Glossary

abolitionist (aa-buh-LIH-shuh-nist) someone who worked to abolish slavery before the Civil War.

adobe (uh-DOH-bee) a brick made of clay mixed with straw and dried in the sun; a building made with these bricks.

affiliations (uh-FIH-lee-AY-shuns) connections with something or somebody.

anthology (an-THAH-luh-jee) a collection of poems or stories by different writers that are all printed in the same book.

armory (AR-muh-ree) a place where weapons are stored.

autobiography (aw-toh-bye-AH-gruh-fee) a book in which the author tells the story of his or her life.

bourgeoisie (boor-zhwah-ZEE) a member of the middle class, with its own conventional ideas and tastes; often used contemptuously.

communism (KAH-myuh-nih-zum) a way of organizing a country so that all the land, houses, and businesses belong to the government or community, and the profits are shared by all.

controversy (KON-truh-ver-see) a discussion marked by opposing views; an argument.

copyrights (KAH-pee-ryts) rights to produce, publish, or sell a song, book, or other written work; requires that others must obtain permission to copy or perform the material.

croissant (krah-SAHN) a rich, crescent-shaped bread roll.

czarist (ZAR-ist) referring to an emperor of Russia before the 1917 revolution.

dialect (DYE-uh-lekt) a way a language is spoken.

frenetic (freh-NEH-tik) frantic, frenzied.

innovation (ih-noh-VAY-shun) a new idea or invention.

interracial (in-tur-RAY-shul) for, of, among, or between races or people of different races.

interred (in-TERD) buried in the earth or in a tomb.

itemized (EYE-tuh-myzd) listed individual items as an account.

malaria (muh-LAY-ree-uh) a tropical disease people get from mosquito bites.

melodramatic (meh-luh-druh-MAH-tik) overly dramatic, sentimental, or emotional.

migration (mye-GRAY-shun) the movement from one country or region to another.

mulatto (myoo-LAH-toh) a person whose ancestry includes both African Americans and Caucasians.

patron (PAY-trun) someone who gives money to or helps another person, an activity, or a cause.

phonograph (FOH-nuh-graf) an early type of record player.

progressive (pruh-GREH-siv) in favor of improvement, progress, or reform.

prose (PROHZ) ordinarily written or spoken language as opposed to verse or poetry.

Renaissance (REH-nuh-zahns) the revival of art and learning in Europe between the 14th and 16th centuries.

sacrilegious (sah-kruh-LIH-jus) disrespectful toward something holy or important.

segregation (seh-gruh-GAY-shun) the act or practice of keeping people or groups apart.

socialism (SOH-shuh-lih-zum) an economic system in which the production of goods is controlled to a high degree by the government.

troubadour (TROO-buh-door) a lyric poet of the eleventh to thirteenth centuries; a wandering musician.

Index